THE MOSES FACTOR

Life and Leadership Lessons for Unlikely Leaders

RUBEN TORRES

Endorsements

The Moses Factor is a powerful and timely book that speaks directly to the heart of leadership, faith, and perseverance. Ruben has crafted an inspiring work that not only re-examines the journey of Moses with fresh perspective, but also equips today's readers with practical lessons for navigating life's challenges and stepping boldly into their purpose. This book is filled with wisdom, clarity, and encouragement, reminding us that with vision, resilience, and faith, we too can rise to meet the call on our lives. I wholeheartedly endorse The Moses Factor and believe it will bless, challenge, and empower everyone who reads it. - **Mark Christopher Lawrence, Emmy Nominated Actor/Comedian**

This book is scars and scripture, proof that God uses the ones everyone else counted out. Leaders listen up: if you're still breathing, you're still chosen. This book is raw, real, and needed for the trenches of ministry. Ruben reminds us that broken doesn't mean done, it means God's just getting started. Leaders limp, but they still lead, and this book shows you how. I've known Ruben for over 20 years, and he has lived every word in these pages." - **Pastor Bo Herroz**

"Ruben Torres speaks straight to the heart of those called to lead through pain, purpose, and perseverance. The Moses Factor reminds every broken leader that God still raises deliverers from the streets, and that our scars can become the blueprint for freedom." - **Dr. Robert Ornelas, Former U.S. Vice Presidential Candidate • Frontman of The S.O.G. Crew (Thump Records / Universal Music Group) • Administrator for the Texas Band of Yaqui Indians to the United Nations**

Ruben! The man of the hour! I've seen Ruben go from street kid, mastering the "Music" game to mature "Man" of God being an example of Loving your neighbor - **Pastor Phil "Chief" Aguilar, Set Free**

I've known Ruben Torres for almost thirty years, and when I think back on our friendship, one memory always comes to mind. When I was first starting out in music, back when nobody knew the name KJ-52, Ruben believed in me. He invested in my career when he had nothing to gain from it, showing me a kind of unselfish support that has marked his life and leadership ever since. That's who Ruben is, someone who sees potential in people long before the spotlight ever does.

Over the years, I've watched him pour that same heart into his community, his ministry, and his family. Whether it's through founding the Love Thy Neighbor Movement, working with artists and leaders, or simply showing up for those who feel forgotten, Ruben has always been about lifting others up. He's never chased titles or platforms, he's chased people, relationships, and the chance to make a difference.

That's why The Moses Factor is such a special book. It's not just a leadership manual, it's a story of redemption, scars, and faith lived out in real time. Ruben knows what it feels like to be overlooked, unqualified, or broken, and yet he's proof that God uses the unlikely to do the extraordinary. Just like Moses, he's learned that leadership isn't about perfection, it's about obedience, humility, and a willingness to let God work through our weakness.

This book carries the same unselfish spirit that Ruben showed me decades ago. It's full of hard-earned wisdom, encouragement for the weary, and a reminder that your story isn't disqualified, it's exactly what God can use.

I've admired Ruben for a long time, and I believe the words you're about to read will challenge you, inspire you, and remind you that you too are called, no matter how unqualified you may feel. **- KJ52 AKA Jonah Sorrentino, Musician/Pastor**

Dedication

First and always, thank You, Lord, for hearing my heart and the desire to put this together. You get all the glory. None of this means anything without You. Thank You for trusting me to speak, to lead, and to write. Your fingerprints are still on everything I do.

To my wife Rosalinda, my Boricua Beauty, I love you with my whole heart. You've put up with all my madness, late nights, wild dreams, and kingdom ideas. You've believed in me when I didn't even believe in myself. Thank you for being my rock and my balance. Thank you for your encouragement and your push to get this book done.

To my kids, Vienna, Benicio, and Gianni - I love you guys so much. You are my legacy. Everything I do is with you in mind. May you walk in even greater things than me. Never forget who you are and who you belong to.

To the other side of my family - The Martinez and Garcia families that have been there for me and my family when we have needed you all the most. The Villalobos, and the Herroz families that were instrumental in one of the most crucial times of my life. I will never forget that!

To my Pops, my brothers Charlie and Edgar and sisters Adriana, Mirna and Nancy - thank you for being part of the fabric of who I am. We've been through it, and we're still standing. To my brother Richie and my Mom who we all miss so much, thank you for your love, your prayers, and your sacrifice.

To all my LTN partners, the Connected men's group, my street fam and LOC MOB brothers who've stood beside me in all my crazy ideas and God-sized dreams, thank you. To my MCWE / Legacy crew that have continued to support and pray for our family. And all those who continue to sharpen me, pray for me, and hold my arms up when I'm tired, you know who you are. I couldn't do this without you. The Zaragozas, The Sandovals, Memo, Kuya, Joey, EZ, Jason Page, Sgt Amado, Tim H, Kellerman, Ricardo & Araceli. This book is ours.

Let's keep building, keep leading, and keep pointing people to Jesus. Stay CONNECTED to the vine, stay CONNECTED to Jesus! - Ruben Torres

Foreward

Sonny Sandoval

Some books you read with your mind. This one you will feel in your bones.

I've known Ruben Torres all of my life. I've seen him in rooms most church folks never walk into, and on stages most church folks only see on YouTube. I've watched him navigate the streets, the music industry, business, and ministry. I've seen him in victory and in heartbreak, in bold faith and in honest questions. So when I tell you this book is real, I don't mean "real" like a catchy slogan. I mean real like scars, late-night prayers, and tears nobody posts on Instagram.

The Moses Factor is not a polished leadership manual written from a safe distance. It's a raw, faith-driven journey for people who don't feel like they belong in the leadership section at all. If you've ever felt too broken to lead… too unqualified to be called… too overlooked to be chosen… this book is for you.

Moses' story is not the story of a perfect leader. It's the story of a fearful, hesitant, messy man with a past, who kept walking with God anyway. And that's exactly why Ruben is the right person to write this. His own life mirrors that tension: born in Tijuana, raised in Southtown, shaped by the streets, refined in the music industry, and then launched into ministry and community leadership.

Ruben has never had the luxury of "theory only." His classroom has been broken neighborhoods, restless green rooms, community events, and quiet hospital visits. His textbooks have been Scripture, disappointment, second chances, and the steady, stubborn grace of God. When he talks about leadership, he's not coming from a conference stage first - he's coming from the concrete.

What I love most about this book is that it doesn't separate "Bible Moses" from "real life you." Ruben weaves the ancient story of Moses together with his own story - his failures, his fears, his missteps, and the moments where God met him right in the middle of his mess. It's scripture and scars on the same page.

As you read, you won't meet a superhero; you'll meet a stuttering, reluctant, easily frustrated man who kept showing up, and a God who refused to let his weaknesses disqualify his calling. That's the heart of The Moses Factor: not that God uses the strongest, the cleanest, or the most put-together, but that He delights in using the unlikely.

Ruben writes with the voice of a brother, not a brand. He doesn't lecture from a distance; he walks beside you. You'll feel that in the way he tells stories, admits his own struggles, and brings Moses off the stained-glass window and into real life. You'll recognize yourself in the doubt, the anger, the insecurity, and you'll also recognize God in the way He keeps showing up in all of it.

I've watched my brother lead when nobody was clapping, serve when nobody was watching, and pour into others when his own cup was empty. We've done men's retreats together where God broke grown men down to tears. We've stood side by side doing ministry, not because we had it all figured out, but because we know what it's like to be the unlikely ones that God still calls.

If you're reading this book, prepare to be challenged. Ruben's gonna make you laugh, make you think, and probably make you uncomfortable. He's gonna remind you that God still uses broken people like us to do some crazy beautiful things, and that your past doesn't cancel your purpose. That leadership starts in the dirt, not on a stage.

In a world full of uncertainty and insecurity, The Moses Factor is a declaration that God is not done with you. It's hope for dreamers who doubt, and for the overlooked who are still chosen. It's a hand on your shoulder saying, "Keep going. Your wilderness is not the end of the story."

Don't rush through these chapters. Let them confront you, comfort you, and call you forward. Let Moses' journey-and Ruben's-give you permission to be honest about where you are, and bold about where God is taking you.

If you've ever wondered, "Can God really use someone like me?" Turn the page. You're about to find out that the answer is yes.

So yeah, from one Southtown original to another, I can tell you this: The Moses Factor ain't just a book, it's a calling. - Sonny Sandoval

Lead Vocalist, P.O.D. Friend, Brother, and Fellow Unlikely Leader

Contents

Contents

Introduction

The Moses Factor

It's NOT about you. Let's get that out of the way right now. Leadership is NEVER about you. That might sting a little, but it's the truth. Once you get that into your head, everything else starts to make sense. Get over yourself. A leader is a person, but leadership is the action that person does. Real leadership should never be about the spotlight, it's about others and empowering the growth of others. When you start doing things for others, that's when you begin to discover who YOU are in Christ.

This book is for the *"Unlikely Leaders"*. For ones who doubt themselves. For the ones who keep their insecurities silent but still wrestle with them at night. For anyone feeling like they don't *fit in* anywhere but are looking for their tribe. It's for the homie locked up in a cell who feels like his purpose is gone. For the single mom trying to raise kids and hold it all together. For the businessman grinding but wondering if his work even matters. For the pastor feeling like a fraud behind the pulpit. For anybody who's ever thought, "Maybe I was built for more, but I just don't see it."

I pray you see what I found… what God can do through a flawed man, and the question, "Who am *I* that I should…?"

Before we get into the "Who Am *I*?" side of things, I need to tell you who I am and why I wrote this.

I grew up in South San Diego with a tight crew of friends, Paco, WUV, Chuck, Sonny, BJ, TJ, Maui, Mikeski, Big Oscar, Hiram, Lil Oscar, Frankie, Shocker, Miguel, Chris. We were a band of brothers. Different gifts, different vibes, but the same kind of influence. People used to tell us we were gonna be world changers. Real talk, we didn't see that. We just knew we had pull and influence. We led others, but not always in the right direction.

To learn more about that you can pick up Sonny Sandoval's book, "Son Of Southtown". We had that influence, but let's be real, we used it the wrong way plenty of times. We loved to party. I led people down the wrong path, getting high, wild parties, criminal activities and I didn't realize the damage until I saw my little brother and nephew following my lead. That's when conviction hit.

Then in 1996, I lost my older brother to that crime-life. A little over a year later, I lost my mom, her heart was broken from the grief of losing my brother with no closure. Those back-to-back hits could have destroyed me. I could have chased revenge. I could have drowned myself in drugs or liquor. But God held me. Even when I didn't know it.

Truth is, I kept running back to the easy money. Helping my boys move weight. Delivering cash and dope. I felt like a hypocrite. I hated what it was, but I wanted the quick cash. Maybe you know that feeling, knowing it's wrong but doing it anyway.

Even as I lived recklessly, I knew something was different in me. I couldn't shake it. That "something" was the call of God, but I ignored it. I had a little video show, rubbing shoulders with celebs, living that party life. And yet, after every wild night, I still felt empty. No matter how fun it looked, I was miserable inside.

Then came my **Moses Factor moment**. I was at a crossroads in life battling depression from divorce and losing my family. On an eight hour drive from San Diego to Modesto, static on the radio except for one Christian station. Pastor Tony Evans was preaching about Moses turning 40 and having to decide who he really was. That hit me like a brick. Moses had to decide: stay in the palace with comfort and sin, or step into his calling and be who God made him.

Right there on the side of the highway, I pulled over and ugly-cried. I felt like God was speaking to me right there about my own personal crossroads. Do I keep up the fake life I was living or do I respond to my calling, to my burning bush? I cried out, "what do you want me to do?" I heard a voice tell me, *"go get your family back"*. Shocked and confused, I was like' *"what did I just hear?"* Then I heard it again. *"Go get your family back"*.

I argued with God for a bit and gave all the reasons why I couldn't go get my family back, until I just caved-in and said, "I'll do whatever you ask me to do", and made my way to start my assignment.

God never said it was going to be an easy assignment, He just said to do it! So, I responded and made my way to Modesto to get my family back! It wasn't easy, but God made a way, softened hearts, restored love, gave us forgiving hearts, and made ways for new beginnings. We are now re-married, and started new with God in the center.

Hebrews 11:24-25 says, "By faith Moses, when he had grown up, refused to be called the son of Pharaoh's daughter, choosing rather to be mistreated with the people of God than to enjoy the fleeting pleasures of sin."

That was scripture that wrecked me. Moses gave up the fake life to walk in his real one. And that's where this book comes from. From me realizing I had to stop running and answer when God called. Like Moses at the burning bush, all I could say was, ***"Here I am."***

Then life threw me another curveball. In my forties, I found out the man I thought was my dad wasn't really my biological father. That news rocked me. Identity crisis, straight up. But my dear friend that had spiritually mentored me, Bo Herroz told me something I'll never forget: he says, *"No matter what that DNA test says, nothing in the world can change who God created you to be. Your Heavenly Father defines you. He gave you the family you have, your heart, your personality, and your purpose and your calling, and no DNA results can ever change that."*

Boom! That's it. That's what I needed to hear to pull me out of confusion and mixed emotions. He finished off by saying, *"It doesn't matter who you are, it matters Whose you are!"*

See, our identity doesn't come from bloodlines or last names. It comes from our heavenly Father. And you've got a purpose bigger than any pain you've been through.

So listen, I'm no Bible scholar, and I won't pretend to be. I'm not gonna hit you with big churchy words. This was a journey of studying biblical leadership through Moses and looking at his story through a different perspective. So yeah, I don't know it all. I'm not even an expert in business leadership. But I am an expert in getting back up after a fall. I know what it's like to have nothing. I know the pain of wasted talent. I know the frustration of self-doubt, imposter syndrome, and thinking you're not good enough. That's why I had to write this, because that's me, I am also an *"Unlikely Leader."*

How many dreams get buried because somebody feels unworthy? How many businesses never get started because someone thinks they don't have what it takes? How many leaders give up because of their past? How many of us don't take that first step towards our dream because fear paralyzes us? That ends now!

Each chapter and each subject are things that took me years to gather together as I wasn't even sure what I was doing when I pieced them together. I pray that these perspectives and nuggets of what I learned in my deep-dive on Moses helps you see what I saw: a flawed, broken, insecure man who God still used in powerful ways. If God can use Moses, He can use me. He can definitely use you.

This book ain't about making Moses into some superhero. Jesus is the ultimate Leader, no question. But Moses' life shows us that even messed-up people can lead when they say yes to God. Moses spent forty years thinking he was somebody, forty years learning he was nobody, and forty years discovering what God can do with a *nobody*.

And that's the journey I want to take you on in these pages. To show you that leadership isn't about fame, power, or titles. It's about *others*. It's about being faithful to your calling. It's about saying, *"Here I am,"* when God calls your name.

If you're ready, let's walk through this together. Leaders on the block, behind bars, in the boardroom, or behind the pulpit, this one's for you. I've added a few components to these chapters that I hope enhance the few nuggets of encouragement that I'm sharing.

The "Handle That" section is a quick challenge that you can take if you feel led. The "Take Note" section is for those that like to journal their walk with the Lord. The last one is "Take it to God", a quick prayer that I hope helps draw you closer to Jesus as you wrap up these chapters.

Chapter 1

The Moses Factor

"So Moses took his wife and sons, put them on a donkey and started back to Egypt. And he took the staff of God in his hand."
- (Exodus 4:20 NIV)

Life and Leadership Lesson

That verse right now may seem pretty random and may not have much meaning to most, but to me, that is the moment I realized Moses had his own 'Moses Factor". He acted on his calling, he moved on what he was supposed to do.

I'm gonna keep it real with you from the jump. I ain't no Bible scholar. I didn't go to seminary, I don't got letters after my name or a fancy title, and I'm not here to impress you with Hebrew or Greek definitions. That's not me. What I do have is a story, and scars, and some nuggets of what I picked up while walking out what I call my Moses Factor.

Here's what I mean. God had already called Moses at the burning bush. But in Exodus 4:20, something shifted. Moses actually packed up his wife, his kids, threw them on a donkey, grabbed the only thing he had, a staff, and started walking toward Egypt. That was the moment. Not when God called him, but when Moses actually moved towards his assignment.

That moment right there, that is the Moses Factor. Hearing is one thing, but acting on it? That's different. That's where *destiny* starts to unfold.

See, some of us have been called already. You know it. God tugged at your heart. Maybe it was in a cell late at night when it was just you and your thoughts. Maybe it was when everyone else counted you out, but you still felt something deep down saying, "You ain't done yet." Maybe it was when someone you didn't expect spoke life into you. You felt it. But feeling it and moving on it are two different games.

Moses didn't roll out with an army and a squad with swords. He didn't have resources stacked. He just had his family and a stick. Crazy, right? That's leadership. Not waiting for the perfect setup, but moving with what you got, trusting that God will show up.

I had my own "Moses Factor" moment. For me, it was when I stopped running from what God was calling me to do. I wasn't perfect. I wasn't polished. I was still dealing with my own junk, still doubting myself. But I couldn't shake that call. At some point, I had to stop saying "one day" and just start walking.

And let's be real. That's you too. What's God been telling you to do that you keep dodging? To lead your family different? To break a cycle? To mentor the younger homies instead of watching them crash? To use your pain, your story, your scars to help somebody else? You can't just sit on it forever. You can't keep waiting for the perfect moment.

Here's the truth: leadership is messy. You're never gonna feel fully ready. But the power isn't in being perfect, it's in showing up. Moses didn't know every step of the plan, but he trusted the One who called him. That's where you gotta land too.

Handle That

Stop waiting on perfect conditions. Stop waiting until you "got it all together." You might never feel ready. Move with what's in your hand today. Write that letter. Make that call. Pray the prayer. Start the conversation. Pack up your donkey and get going.

Take Note

- What's the assignment God's been putting on your heart, but you've been stalling on?
- What excuses have you been using to keep from moving forward?
- If you had to name your "staff", the one thing God's already given you, what would it be?

Take It to God

Father, I don't want to waste time waiting for perfect. I know You've already called me. Give me the courage to step out even when I don't feel ready. Help me see what You've already put in my hand, and trust that You can do more with it than I ever could. No more excuses. Today I'm moving with You. In Jesus' Name, Amen.

Who Do I Think I Am?

"But Moses said to God, 'Who am I that I should go to Pharaoh and bring the Israelites out of Egypt?" - (Exodus 3:11 NIV)

Life and Leadership Lesson

This one hits different because I've asked the same question Moses asked. Maybe you have too. God called Moses, and instead of saying "bet, let's roll," his first response was, *"Who am I?"* Like, for real God? Me? You sure You didn't mean the guy next to me?

That's how we think. Who am I to start that business? Who am I to lead my family different when I've messed it up so many times already? Who am I to step into ministry when people still remember my old life? Who am I to think God could actually use me when I don't even feel qualified to lead myself?

Sound familiar? "Who am I, that I should...?"

Start a podcast? Lead a nonprofit? Speak in front of law enforcement when I used to dodge 'em? Act in films? Write this book?

And God reminded me: "I will give you the words.", "I already placed something in your hand.", "You're not going alone."

This book? This is my answer to that question. This is my "yes."

Here's the thing. Moses wasn't wrong about his flaws. Dude had a record. He killed a man back in Egypt. He ran away. He spent 40 years hiding in the desert, raising sheep, not exactly a résumé that screams "future national leader." But God still called him. And the fact that Moses questioned it makes his story that much more like ours.

I can't even count how many times I've asked God the same thing. "Who am *I* that You'd trust me with this vision? Who am *I* to lead when I've made my share of mistakes? Who am *I* to speak into people's lives when I still feel broken myself?" Who am *I* to go talk to inmates at a prison when I've never even been locked up? And every time, God reminds me, it was never about *who I am*, it's about *who He is*.

That's the key right there. You'll disqualify yourself a hundred times over if you keep looking at your past, your record, your weaknesses, or the labels people slapped on you. Some of you reading this know exactly what it feels like when your name comes up in a courtroom, in the streets, or even at church, and people only see your past. But God doesn't introduce you by your rap sheet. He introduces you by your purpose.

So, whose voice are you listening to? The voice of your doubt? The voice of people who've judged you? Or God's voice who says, "I chose you"?

Leaders aren't chosen because they're flawless. They're chosen because they're willing. Your pain, your scars, your experiences, that's your seminary. That's your leadership training ground. And the moment you say yes, God flips the script.

So, who do you think you are? Better yet, who does God say you are? That right there is the most important thing about you! Your identity in Christ.

Handle That

Write down every label people ever used against you, convict, dropout, addict, screw-up, failure, and then cross them out one by one. Replace them with what God calls you: chosen, son, daughter, forgiven, blessed, leader.

Take Note

- What's the "Who am *I*?" question you keep asking God?
- When you think of your past, what lies do you tell yourself that make you feel unqualified?
- How would your life shift if you believed God's identity for you over the one the world gave you?

Take It to God

Father, I admit I've doubted myself. I've questioned my calling. I hate that I've let my past and other people's opinions define me. But today I choose to believe what You say about me. Help me walk in my true identity as Your child, called and chosen, even when I don't feel worthy. Remind me that my confidence comes from who You are, not who I am. In Jesus' Name, Amen.

Send Someone Else

"But Moses said, 'Pardon your servant, Lord. Please send someone else." -
Exodus 4:13 (NIV)

Life and Leadership Lesson

Moses really said straight up, ***"God, send someone else."*** Think about that. The God of the universe shows up in fire, calls him by name, lays out the assignment, and Moses still tried to tap out. Sounds wild, right? But let's be real. Haven't you done the same?

"God, send someone else to step up and speak." "God, send someone else to start that ministry." "God, send someone else to lead my family." "God, send someone else to go into those streets or that prison and talk to the ones nobody else will touch."

We all get tempted to pass on the assignment. Why? Because leadership costs something. It's uncomfortable. It makes you face your insecurities. And sometimes it feels easier to just let somebody else do it.

But here's what we miss when we say, *"Send someone else."* We miss the giant that was meant for us.

Look at David. His dad didn't send him to the battlefield to be a warrior. He sent him to be an errand boy, delivering bread and cheese to his brothers. If David had said, *"Man, let someone else do it. I ain't nobody's delivery boy,"* he would've missed the exact assignment that positioned him to take down Goliath. That little "yes" to bring food put him in the room where God needed him.

The point is, when God sends YOU, He means it for YOU. Not your brother. Not your homeboy. Not your pastor. Not the dude down the block. YOU. Because there's something tied to your "yes" that only you can release.

I think about all the times I tried to dodge the call. Times when I said, "God, I'm not the right one. Send someone who talks better. Send someone with an education. Send someone with more resources." But God kept pressing: *"Nah, Ruben. I chose you."*

And He's saying the same to you. If you keep pushing it off, you're not just delaying your own growth, you might be robbing someone else of the breakthrough they're supposed to get through your obedience.

So, let me ask you: where in your life are you still telling God to send someone else? What giant are you missing because you don't want to carry the bread and cheese assignment first?

Be honest, how many times have you done the same?

We act like dodging the call will make the weight disappear. But here's the truth: when God calls you, He means *you*. Not your brother. Not your pastor. Not your cellie. Not the more polished dude down the street. YOU.

Look at David. His big moment didn't come when he was crowned king. It came when his dad told him to take bread and cheese to his brothers on the battlefield. That was a low-level assignment, basically an errand boy move. But David didn't say, *"Send someone else."* He said yes. And because he said yes, he was standing in the exact spot where Goliath was taunting God's people. If he dodged that "small" job, he might've missed the giant that changed his life forever.

That's the lesson. Some of the biggest opportunities you'll ever have won't look big at first. They'll look small, ordinary, even beneath you. But those "bread and cheese" moments are what position you for the giants.

Leadership isn't always about saying yes to the big stage. It's about saying yes to the small assignments, trusting God will use them to set you up for the bigger ones. Sometimes it's about serving in the kids ministry and not always needing to be on stage with a mic in your hand preaching.

So let me ask you: what have you been saying "send someone else" to? Is it your family? Your community? A calling that feels too heavy? A vision you've been running from? What giant might you be missing because you refuse to carry bread and cheese first?

Maybe you didn't say it out loud, but your actions said it. You sat on the gift. You held back the idea. You kept quiet when you should have spoken. You passed on the opportunity because you were scared of messing it up. Be real with yourself.

Don't dodge it. When God called you, He knew your flaws. He knew your record. He knew your struggles. And He still picked you. That's not by accident. And when you think you're not enough He sends you a helper.

Then the Lord became angry with Moses. 'All right,' he said. 'What about your brother, Aaron the Levite? I know he speaks well. And look! He is on his way to meet you now. He will be delighted to see you.' - (Exodus 4:14 NLT)

Crazy right? Moses went from "I can't talk" to "Send someone else." He straight up tried to dodge his assignment. And God got heated. But even in His anger, God provided backup through Aaron. That's wild. God could have just dropped Moses right there, but He didn't. Why? Because when God calls, He already sees the end from the beginning. He doesn't call you because you are perfect, He calls you because He has a purpose

The truth is, God can use anyone. He used Pharaoh's daughter to save baby Moses. He used a donkey to talk sense into Balaam (Numbers 22:28-30). He used fishermen who smelled like the sea and tax collectors who were hated by everybody to flip the world upside down (Matthew 4:19, Mark 2:14). He used a kid with five loaves and two fish to feed thousands (John 6:9-13). He even used a widow with just a little oil to show His power (2 Kings 4:1-7).

Who do you think is too far gone that God can't use? What if God is calling you to be the one to reach them? How many lives are waiting on your obedience?

The whole Bible screams this truth: God is not limited by who you are or where you come from. He is only limited when you refuse to say yes. Boom. That's it.

Peep this.

- If you are locked up reading this, do not believe the lie that your life is over. God can use you in that cell to lead other men to Him.
- If you are a business owner, don't think God only uses pastors. He can use you in boardrooms and at job sites to make an impact in the market place.

- If you are a single mom hustling to raise your kids, God can use you right there in your home to raise up leaders for the next generation.
- If you are a pastor or ministry leader, don't overlook the ones who seem "least likely." They may be your Aaron, sent to walk beside you.

See, when you reject the call, you don't just hurt yourself, you rob others of what God wanted to do through you. Moses wanted to push it off, but if he had, millions of Israelites would have been left in Egypt. Like I said in the very beginning…leadership is never just about you. Somebody is counting on your "yes".

The kingdom does not move on excuses. It moves on obedience. God can use anyone, but will you let Him use you?

Handle That

Stop dodging the call. Today, decide to step into the assignment of an *unlikely leader* that God gave you, big or small. Don't wait for the *giant* moment. Be faithful in the *"bread and cheese"* moments, because that's where God sets you up for the big victories.

Take Note

- What *giant* could be waiting on the other side of your obedience?
- Where in your life have you been telling God, "send someone else"?
- What *"bread and cheese"* assignment are you overlooking that might be leading to your giant moment?

Take It to God

Father, forgive me for all the times I've tried to dodge the call and push it onto someone else. I see now that when You call, You mean me. Even when the assignment feels small or heavy, help me to be faithful. Teach me not to despise small beginnings or low-level tasks, because I know they lead to greater purpose. Give me courage to step up, even when I feel unqualified. If You called me, You'll go with me. I say yes to what You're asking.I admit that sometimes I want to say, "Send someone else." I don't always feel ready, and I don't always feel strong enough. But today, I choose to believe that You can use anyone, even me. Remove my excuses. Help me to see others the way You see them, not by their past or their flaws, but by their potential in You. Thank You for not giving up on me. In Jesus' Name, Amen

Chapter 2

Supposed to Be Dead… But Here I Am

"Then Pharaoh gave this order to all his people: 'Every Hebrew boy that is born you must throw into the Nile, but let every girl live." - (Exodus 1:22 NIV)

Life and Leadership Lesson

Moses should have never made it out the gate. A government order on his head before he could crawl. His parents hid him for three months, then put him in a basket and slid him into a river knowing God would take care of him. That little basket floated past death and landed in Pharaoh's house. Protected and provided for, Crazy.

Let's keep it real. Some of us got that same story in a different outfit. You were supposed to be dead too. Wrong block, wrong night, wrong crowd. That overdose that should have cooked your heart. That wreck you walked away from while the car looked like a crushed soda can. That fight, that riot, that yard, that alley. I've been there.

I was in a few car accidents, I was shot at, I've been in a few rumbles. I should have been a RIP post. I should have been a mural on a wall in South San Diego. But here I am. Not luck, purpose.

I remember when I got out of the hospital after my first really bad car accident, my pops told me that the only reason I was alive was because God spared me for a reason and I better figure out what that reason is and I better start living better because I was close to meeting him.

When God spares you, He is speaking without words. He is telling you, I am not finished with you. Moses wasn't saved so he could flex that palace life. He was saved to lead people out. Your survival is not a trophy, it is an assignment. It's a second chance at doing things right, making things right, and living right.

The Bible is full of "supposed to be dead, but here I am" stories:

- **Baby Jesus** survived Herod's hit list when Joseph was warned in a dream and moved the family to Egypt, purpose protected purpose (**Matthew 2:13-16**).
- **Joash** was a baby target too, hidden by his aunt from a murderous queen, then raised to be king at the right time (**2 Kings 11:1-3**).
- **Daniel** should have been lion food, God shut mouths (**Daniel 6:16-23**).
- **Shadrach, Meshach, Abednego** should have been ash, they walked out without smoke on their clothes (**Daniel 3:23-27**).
- **David** should have been a dead man with Saul's spear in his back, God kept making a way out of caves and ambushes (**1 Samuel 23-24**).
- **Paul** was stoned, left for dead, shipwrecked, snake-bit, and still kept it moving because the mission wasn't done (**Acts 14:19-20, Acts 27, Acts 28:3-6**).

- **Peter** was chained between guards, but the angel walked him out like it was a morning stroll (**Acts 12:6-11**).

What about you? What should have killed you, but didn't? Why do you think God kept you breathing? If the enemy came at you that hard, what does he see in you that you are still sleeping on?

Leaders, this hits all lanes. If you run a business, your second chance means steward people and resources with fear of God, not fear of failure. If you pastor or lead spiritually, your survival story is a sermon somebody needs. If you're locked up, you're "still here" and it's proof of God's call. If you are a mom or dad trying to hold it together, your breath this morning is fresh mercy to lead your home with love and courage.

Moses' survival wasn't random. It set him up to confront the system that tried to drown him. That might be your play too. The place you almost died is often the place God will use you to bring life. Your calling is where pain and passion collide.

You survived addiction, now you help others get free. You survived the streets, now you mentor the next generation off the corner. You survived church hurt, now you build a healthy community. You survived financial collapse, now you teach money wisdom. You survived abuse, now you're walking someone else through their freedom. Boom, that's wild, but it's real.

Ask yourself:

- What did God carry me through that I used to be ashamed to talk about?
- Who needs the hope I'm hiding?
- If I stood up today and owned my story, who would find the courage to stand up with me?

"For many are called, but few are chosen" (Matthew 22:14 NLT). The call is going out to everybody, but the chosen are the ones who answer and obey. God expects the called to respond, to repent, to grow, to serve, to lead. Not perfect, but available. Not famous, but faithful. Moses said, "Here I am," then he kept saying yes, step after shaky step, shepherd staff in hand.

So what are you doing with your second chance at life? Are you drifting back to the old hustle, or are you building what God spared you to build? What have you done with the grace that God provided to get you out of that situation that only He could have got you out of? Are you playing small, or are you stepping into the assignment? Take it easy with the excuses, for real. If God kept you, He will equip you. If He preserved you, He will position you. Your survival is a signal. Answer it.

Handle That

- Write out **three moments** you know should have taken you out. Next to each, write, **"But here I am."** Sit with that, marinate in that goodness and grace.
- Tell one trusted person your survival story this week. Don't polish it, just tell it.
- Do one act of unlikely leadership tied to your story. Call the young homie who is slipping. Apply for the program. Start the support group. Book the counseling. Make the move.

Take Note

- What exact moment do you know God spared your life? Describe it in detail.
- What lies did you believe about yourself because of your past, and what truth is God speaking now?
- If your survival equals assignment, what is one step of obedience you can take in the next 72 hours?

Take It to God

Father, thank You for keeping me when I should have been gone. Thank You for yanking me out of wrecks, bullets, bad decisions, and dark seasons. I know You spared me for a reason. Show me the assignment tied to my survival. Give me courage to speak my story, wisdom to lead with humility, and love to serve the people You put in front of me. I am still here, so use me. **In Jesus' Name, Amen.**

Chapter 3

Drawn Out for a Reason

"When the child grew older, she took him to Pharaoh's daughter and he became her son. She named him Moses, saying, 'I drew him out of the water."
- (Exodus 2:10 NIV)

Life and Leadership Lesson

Names mean something. Don't ever think they don't. Why do you think people don't name their son Judas? In the Bible, a name wasn't just what your mama yelled when you were in trouble, it carried weight, identity, destiny. Sometimes our name is all we have. **Proverbs 22:1** says *"A good name is more desirable than great riches; to be esteemed is better than silver or gold."*

Where I'm from, your name and reputation is everything. Ask yourself, when people out in the community hear your name, what crosses their mind? What's the first thing they think when they hear your name? *"Oh, that dude? Naw, I'm good, I ain't trying to hang with him!"* Or is there excitement and people love having you around. So trust me, protect your name, protect your reputation because that social currency will come in handy some day.

I've worked hard to maintain my name in good standing everywhere I go, because it means something. But what if God changes your name? I'm not talking about a funny nickname, like a big dude being called Tiny. I'm talking about a name with purpose, and meaning for his glory.

Let's see what the word says: Abram became Abraham, father of nations (**Genesis 17:5**). Jacob became Israel, the one who wrestled with God and walked with a limp (**Genesis 32:28**). Simon became Peter, the rock Jesus would build His church on (**Matthew 16:18**). Saul became Paul, transformed from a killer of Christians to an apostle of Christ (**Acts 9**).

And then we get to Moses. Pharaoh's daughter gives him the name *Moses* because she drew him out of the water. But let's look closer, that name wasn't just about one river rescue. That name was prophetic. That name *was* purpose. His whole life was about being drawn out, and drawing others out.

Let's break it down real quick. What Moses was *"drawn out of."*

- **Drawn out of death.** Moses was born under a death sentence. Pharaoh had ordered every Hebrew boy drowned and thrown into the Nile. His parents hid him for three months, then trusted God enough to put him in a basket on the Nile. That river was supposed to kill him, but it became the place where God preserved him. You too, how many times were you supposed to be dead but God kept you? What bullets missed you? What overdose didn't finish you? What wreck left you standing? If you're reading this right now, you've been drawn out of death too.

- **Drawn out of the Nile.** The Nile was chaotic, dangerous, full of crocodiles and uncertainty. Yet out of those waters, Moses was lifted up by Pharaoh's daughter. Don't miss that, sometimes God lets you float in the chaos so that when He draws you out, you know it wasn't anybody but Him. What's your Nile? Addiction? Anger? Poverty? Incarceration? Loneliness? Depression? Relationship? What waters did He draw you out of?

- **Drawn out of the palace.** Moses grew up with that palace privilege. Riches, education, royalty. Yet he had to be drawn out of that fake life to step into his real calling. Leaders, let's be honest, what palaces are we clinging to? The palace of comfort, money, fake followers on social media, approval of people? Sometimes God draws us out of the palace so we can discover our purpose. Moses couldn't lead slaves while living as a prince. Maybe God is drawing you out of the palace of pretending, so you can lead from authenticity.

- **Drawn out of the wilderness.** Moses ran into the wilderness after killing an Egyptian, thinking his story was done. For 40 years, he was just another shepherd. But even there, God drew him out again. The burning bush moment wasn't just about fire, it was about God saying, "You've been hiding long enough. Time to step up." Ever feel like you've been in hiding? Ever feel like your failures disqualified you? The wilderness isn't wasted. God can draw you out of that too.

And then the biggest one, **Moses drew the people of God out of Egypt.** His whole name was his mission. What he experienced personally, he was called to do for others. That's leadership. God draws you out so you can draw others out.

So let me ask you, what has God drawn you out of? What pit, what addiction, what hustle, what prison, what abusive relationship, what mindset, what situation? And why? Maybe the very thing He pulled you out of is the very thing He wants you to lead others out of.

If He pulled you out of addiction, maybe you're supposed to help others get free. If He drew you out of poverty, maybe you're supposed to create jobs, start businesses, and build community. If He pulled you out of the streets, maybe you're supposed to mentor the next generation.

David was drawn out of shepherd life to be a king (**1 Samuel 16**). Joseph was drawn out of a pit and a prison to lead a nation through famine (**Genesis 41**). Esther was drawn out of obscurity to stand before a king and save her people (**Esther 4**). Jesus Himself drew Peter out of a boat to walk on water (**Matthew 14:29**), and later drew him out of shame after his denial (**John 21:15-17**).

So what's your name? Not just what's on your birth certificate, what has God called you? What label is He trying to peel off of you so you can walk in who He created you to be? Are you letting Him rename you? Are you living up to what He's spoken over your life?

This ain't just about Moses. This is about you, the *unlikely leader.* You've been drawn out. You've been preserved. You were saved for a reason. You've been renamed by God's grace. The question is, now that you're here, what are you gonna do with it?

Handle That

- Write down your name and look up what it means. Ask yourself if your life reflects it or if God is trying to give you a new one.

- List out the things God has drawn you out of. Don't sugarcoat it. Be real, the addictions, the near-deaths, the failures, the medical diagnosis, the seasons of wilderness. Pray over each one and ask God to show you how He wants to use your story to draw other *unlikely leaders* out.

Take Note

- What's your Nile, the place you were supposed to drown but God drew you out?
- What "palace" has God called you out of so you can walk in your real assignment?
- Who in your life needs you to lead them out of the same thing God led you out of?

Take It to God

Father, thank You for calling me by name and drawing me out when I should have been gone. Thank You for pulling me out of my Nile, out of my palace of pretending, out of my wilderness of hiding. Help me not to waste the rescue. Show me how to lead others out of the same traps You led me out of. Give me courage to walk in my true name and live on purpose. **In Jesus' Name, Amen.**

Chapter 4

The Shepherd Season

"Now Moses was tending the flock of Jethro his father-in-law, the priest of Midian, and he led the flock to the far side of the wilderness and came to Horeb, the mountain of God." - (Exodus 3:1 NIV)

Life and Leadership Lesson

Dang, Moses went from living in Pharaoh's palace to walking behind sheep in the desert. Talk about a downgrade. From gold floors to dirty sandals. From eating at the king's table to smelling like sheep. People probably looked at him like, "What happened to this dude? He fell off."

But here's the crazy part, that's exactly where God wanted him. See, shepherds weren't respected, they were looked down upon. They were the nobodies, the outsiders, the ones that society didn't celebrate, but God would lift them up.

Genesis 46:34 says Egyptians considered shepherds "an abomination."

They were the bottom of the barrel. Dirty. Overlooked. Not influencers. Unlikely leaders.

But guess who the angels told first when Jesus was born? *Shepherds.* (**Luke 2:8–14**)

God trusted nobodies with the biggest announcement in human history. He keeps choosing shepherds.

Time and time again, God used shepherds to shape leaders. **David** was a shepherd before he was a king. **Jacob** was a shepherd before his family became a nation. Even Jesus called Himself the **Good Shepherd**.

You catch that? God put His greatest leaders in "lowly" jobs before He trusted them with people. Why? Because if you can't care for sheep, then you can't care for souls. If you can't handle dirty, stubborn animals, you won't survive leading stubborn people.

Let's keep it real. Some of you reading this feel like you're in your own shepherd season right now. You're doing work that feels beneath you. The grind nobody notices. The position nobody wants. Maybe you're sweeping floors, clocking in at a job you don't love, sitting in a cell with nothing but time, sweeping up hair at a barbershop, or hustling in ways that don't look glamorous. And you're thinking, "This can't be what God meant for me."

You see…the shepherd season is your training ground. God is teaching you patience and how to handle responsibility. He's teaching you how to lead with care, not ego and how to value the sheep before He gives you the staff to part the sea.

Are you allowing yourself to be a shepherd right now? Or are you despising it, wishing for the spotlight before you've learned the lesson?

Leadership isn't about climbing to the top fast. It's about being faithful in the field. And if God trusted David with sheep before He trusted him with Israel, and if God trusted Moses with sheep before He trusted him with a nation, what makes you think your shepherd season doesn't matter?

The question is, what's God teaching you right here, right now? And are you humble enough to learn it?

Handle That

Instead of complaining about where you are, ask God what He's trying to teach you in this season. Write it down. Own it. Commit to being faithful in the "sheep field" before the "spotlight on a stage."

Take Note

- What's your "sheep field" right now, the place you feel overlooked or stuck in?
- How has God already been shaping your patience, your *unlikely leadership*, or your humility in this season?
- What would change if you stopped despising where you are and started seeing it as training?

Take It to God

Father, thank You for my shepherd season. I may not like it, but I trust that You're using it to shape me. Teach me to be faithful in the quiet, humble places. Remind me that nothing is wasted in Your hands. If You could use shepherds like David, Jacob, and even Moses, then You can use me too. Prepare my heart to lead people by first teaching me how to serve well. Don't let me rush past this season or despise it. Help me to stay patient until You call me to the next level. **In Jesus' Name, Amen.**

Silence Before the Fire

"When Pharaoh heard of this, he tried to kill Moses, but Moses fled from Pharaoh and went to live in Midian, where he sat down by a well." - *(Exodus 2:15 NIV)*

Life and Leadership Lesson

Here's something crazy… Scripture barely says a word about Moses' forty years in Midian. One verse says he sat down by a well, then boom, the next thing you know he's a husband, a shepherd, and forty years older. No miracles. No signs. No big leadership moments. Just silence.

That's wild to me. Because when we read the Bible, we see the highlight reel, the plagues, the Red Sea, the Ten Commandments. But what about the decades that didn't make the highlight reel? What about the quiet seasons nobody writes books about? I mean, he lived 3 chapters of his life, each one was a 40 year chapter. That quiet chapter before he was called to the bush was dead silent.

Moses had forty years of that. Silence. Routine. Obscurity.

And I think some of you feel like that's your life right now. Like, "God, where you at? Why ain't You talking? Why ain't doors opening? Why's it so quiet?" Have you ever been in that spot where it feels like your prayers hit the ceiling and bounce back down? Where life feels like one long Midian desert: sheep, sand, repeat?

The Bible doesn't give us the details of those years, but maybe that's the point. Maybe silence is where God does His deepest work. Maybe that's where He's stripping you of pride, breaking bad habits, removing the addiction, teaching humility, shaping your patience, and sharpening your leadership. Think about it: Moses couldn't lead people out of Egypt until he learned how to lead sheep in Midian. And that takes years, not days.

So let me ask you: what do you do when God is quiet? Do you panic and think He left you? Do you try to fill the silence with noise, chasing money, attention, the party, distractions? Or do you sit with it, knowing that silence doesn't mean absence?

At the time of writing this, it has been four years of my wife battling cancer. We have a ton of people praying for us, we pray together about her health, continue treatment, and do what the doctors ask. I have cried out to God about this all this time and it feels like He is silent, however he continues to show us and provide, we feel His presence, and see him in the situation. We may not hear him at the moment, but we know he has been with us every bit of the way.

The silence is shaping you.

Look at Scripture. **Joseph** sat in prison for years while heaven seemed quiet (**Genesis 39-41**). **David** was anointed king but spent years hiding in caves before he wore the crown (**1 Samuel 24**). **Elijah** hid by a brook in silence until God sent him to confront Ahab (**1 Kings 17**). Even **Jesus** had thirty "silent" years before His ministry started, and between the ages of 12 and 30 there was nothing really even said at all about that quiet time... no miracles, no crowds, just working in His father's shop. God moves in the quiet as much as He does in the fire.

So here's the bigger question: What is God doing when He's quiet? He's preparing you. He's testing your faithfulness when nobody's looking. He's training your hands for the assignment you don't even see coming yet.

And maybe the even harder question: What are YOU doing when He's quiet? Are you still showing up? Are you still praying? Are you still walking in integrity when nobody claps? Because if you can't lead yourself in silence, you won't be able to lead others in the spotlight.

Moses sat in silence for forty years, and then one day, one regular day, there was a bush on fire. That's the pattern. Quiet. Quiet. Quiet. Fire. God often works like that. Long seasons of nothing, then suddenly, everything changes.

So don't despise the silence. Don't rush the waiting. If God seems quiet, it's not because He left. It's because He's working on something in you that can only be built in obscurity.

So let me throw this at you: Will you trust Him in the quiet season? Will you be faithful in your Midian so you'll be ready for your burning bush?

Handle That

- Write down the areas in your life where it feels like God is silent right now.
- Next to each one, write: "Silence isn't absence. God is preparing me."
- This week, choose one way to stay faithful in your "Midian", whether that's prayer, consistency at work, or just staying humble in the grind.

Take Note

- Where do you feel like God is quiet in your life right now?
- How do you usually react in silence? trust or frustration?
- What might God be shaping in you during this silent season that He couldn't teach you in the spotlight?

Take It to God

Father, silence is hard. I want answers fast, I want doors to open, I want the fire. But I know Your timing is different from mine. Teach me to trust You in the quiet season. Remind me that silence doesn't mean You forgot me. Shape me in the hidden places, build my patience, and strengthen my character so I'll be ready when You show up. Help me to see Midian as training, not punishment. Keep me faithful until the fire comes. **In Jesus' Name, Amen.**

Chapter 5

What's in Your Hand?

"Then the LORD said to him, 'What is that in your hand?' 'A staff,' he replied." - (Exodus 4:2 NIV)

Life and Leadership Lesson

This one here is the topic of thousands of sermons from pastors from all over the world so I won't go too deep on this. See, Moses tried to tell God he wasn't ready. He didn't have what it took. And God hit him with a simple question: ***"What's in your hand?"*** Moses looked down and said, "A staff." Just a stick. Something ordinary. Something he'd been carrying around without thinking twice.

But here's the thing, that staff wasn't just a stick anymore. In God's hands it became a tool for miracles. It turned into a snake, it split the Red Sea, it struck a rock and water came out. The same stick he thought was nothing became everything God used to prove His power.

See, in **Exodus 4:2**, it was just a staff. In **Exodus 4:20**, it became The Rod of God because it had power from God.

Now let's talk about you. What's in *your* hand?

We waste so much time focused on what we *don't* have. The money we wish we had. The resources we're missing. But God ain't asking about what you don't got. He's asking, *"What's already in your hand?"*

If you're an entrepreneur or business owner, maybe what's in your hand is an idea, a skill, a hustle, a gift for connecting people. If you're a leader, maybe it's your story, your scars, your ability to relate to people that others can't. For some of you, what's in your hand is time, and you're wasting it. For others, it's influence, and you're not stewarding it.

You remember in the movie **A Bronx Tale** when Robert Deniro's character, Lorenzo encourages his son "C" about wasted talent? He said, **"The saddest thing in life is wasted talent."** That's for real. How many people never use what God already put in their hand because they're too busy wishing for something bigger? They wasted opportunities over making good choices. That's wasted talent. And wasted talent is wasted purpose.

Think about David. When Goliath was standing in front of him, he didn't ask for Saul's armor or beg for a sword. He picked up his slingshot, something simple, something he'd been using since he was a kid. And God used that little weapon to drop a giant.

Or the kid with five loaves and two fish. It looked like nothing compared to feeding thousands. But Jesus took what was in his hand and multiplied it. The miracle wasn't in what they didn't have, it was in what they *did*.

So I'll ask you: what's in your hand right now that you're overlooking? What talent, what resource, what gift are you sitting on while telling God you don't have enough? Are you wasting your talent because it doesn't look flashy or cool? Stop tripping on what everyone may think and just do what God is asking whether you think the cool kids will dig it or not.

Leadership and business both come down to stewardship. God ain't asking you to have everything. He's asking if you'll use the little He already gave you. Because if you're faithful with the little what's in your hand, He'll trust you with more.

Don't let your story be one of wasted talent.

Handle That

Take inventory. Write down the gifts, skills, relationships, and resources you already have. Then circle one you've been sleeping on and decide to put it to work this week. Stop chasing what you don't have and start using what's already in your hand.

Take Note

What talent or gift has God put in your hand that you've been neglecting? Where have you been wasting what you've been given? How would your leadership, your business, or your influence change if you actually used what's already in your hand?

Take It to God

Father, forgive me for wasting what You've already put in my hand. I've spent too much time chasing what I don't have instead of using what I do. Open my eyes to see the gifts, talents, and resources You've trusted me with. Teach me to be faithful, creative, and bold with them. Don't let me waste my talent or miss the giants I could take down with what's already in my hand. Use me to multiply what I've got for Your purpose. **In Jesus' Name, Amen.**

Tabernacle Builders

"All who are skilled among you are to come and make everything the Lord has commanded." - (Exodus 35:10)

Life and Leadership Lesson

The fifth word in the Bible is **"created."** Think about that. God could've started His story with anything, but He wanted us to know right away, He's *the* Creator. And since we're made in His image, that means creativity runs in our DNA too.

When God called Moses to lead the Israelites, He didn't just call Moses alone. God doesn't only work through preachers, warriors, or politicians. He works through *all of us*. In Exodus 35, God called on the skilled, the craftsmen, the builders, the artists, the fashion designers, the woodworkers, the jewelers. The *"Unlikely Leaders"*. He said:

"All who are skilled among you are to come and make everything the Lord has commanded."

Straight up, because it shows that God doesn't just use sermons and swords. He uses the creatives and their skills and talents. He uses people like you and me.

This hits hard because I've spent most of my life around creatives, musicians, designers, filmmakers, producers, writers, painters, DJs. I've been in recording studios, backstage at shows, and inside juvenile halls with kids learning how to rap, paint, or make beats. And you know what I've seen? God shows up in the art. It's a tool that God has used to hook people in.

You might not think of yourself as someone with a "gift" to offer. Maybe you're like, *"I just paint. I just edit videos. I just cut hair. I just build furniture. I just design clothes."* But peep this, God placed that in your hands. And He's saying, **"Use it to build My Kingdom."**

Think about it: Noah built an ark. Saved humanity. David wrote songs that still heal souls today.   Bezalel and Oholiab were literally filled with the Spirit to design the tabernacle, carving, weaving, creating beauty for God's dwelling (**Exodus 31:1-5**).

So let me ask you: What's in your hand? Is it a mic? A spray can? A camera? A sewing machine? Barber clippers and scissors? A pen? A paint brush? A welding torch? That's not random. That's sacred.

I've seen this play out in my own story. Back in the day, when we launched Jefe Clothing, I thought I was just building a brand. But it turned into something way bigger, it became a voice for a culture. It became a way to connect people, inspire them, even point them toward God without them even realizing it.

When I directed music videos and documentaries, I thought I was just capturing their story. But later, I realized I was also capturing *hope*, documenting people's pain, redemption, and their fight to rise above.

When we ran workshops inside juvenile halls, teaching kids how to DJ, rap, or paint, it wasn't just about art. It was discipleship in disguise. Creativity became the bridge for them to see they had worth, they are valued and that they had something God could use.

That's what creativity does, it opens doors that sermons sometimes can't.

But here's where it gets real, your gift isn't just for you. Just like those tabernacle builders weren't making stuff for their own hype, you're not supposed to hoard your gift. You're supposed to offer it back to God. And when you do, it becomes holy.

That mural? That song? That movie? That clothing line? That sculpture you built? If you surrender it to Him, it becomes more than talent. It becomes a tabernacle, a space for God's presence to show up and change lives.

So teach it. Pass it on. When God gives you a gift, it's never just for you. It's meant to multiply. Pour into the next generation. Mentor them. Show them the way.

Now ask yourself, Am I using my gift for clout, or for Kingdom? Am I passing it on, or am I hoarding it? Because creatives, we're called to build too. As you offer your talents to God, ask yourself: How can I use my gift to serve others? How can I build something that points people back to the Creator? There's a place in the kingdom for the singers, the artists, the builders, and the dreamers. I've been into several prisons and hosted art shows inside. You would be amazed at what the homies inside can create from elastic from your underwear, popsicle sticks, and cardboard! No excuses, if they can create with the little they got, you better be stepping your game up!

God is calling you to use what's in your hands, not just for your benefit, but for His glory. And what's powerful here is that God used people with *skills*, not just religious knowledge or political power. He used people with creative gifts, people like us.

Handle That

Take your talent today, whatever it is, and do something on purpose for God. Write that song. Paint that wall. Shoot that video. Design that shirt. Write that book. But don't just make it, dedicate it. Pray over it. Offer it to Him. Then bless someone with it. You're not just an artist. You're not just a builder. You're a tabernacle builder.

Take Note

What has God gifted me to build? Am I creating for hype, or for Him? How can I use my creativity to bless others and point people to Jesus? Who can I pour into so the gift doesn't stop with me? How can I teach others to find purpose in their creativity and serve God with what's in their hands?

Take It To God

Father, thank You for the creativity You've placed in me. I don't want to waste it. I don't want to hoard it. I offer my gifts back to You today. Take my art, my hustle, my vision, make it holy. Let it bless Your people and point them back to You. Help me teach others to do the same. **In Jesus' Name, Amen.**

Chapter 6

The Burning Bush Factor

The Calling

"When the Lord saw that he had gone over to look, God called to him from within the bush, 'Moses! Moses!' And Moses said, 'Here I am."
- (Exodus 3:4 NIV)

Life and Leadership Lesson

Picture this. Moses is just out there in the wilderness, another regular day, same routine, nothing new. He's watching sheep, probably thinking this is all his life is gonna be. Then BOOM!... a bush catches fire but it doesn't burn up. Moses steps closer, curious, and suddenly he hears his own name out of the fire. *"Moses! Moses!"*

That's wild. God didn't say, "Hey you," or "Hey shepherd boy." He called Moses by name. That's personal. That's intentional. That's purpose.

And here's what hits different, God still calls us by name too. He doesn't call you by your case number, your record, your mistakes, or your insecurities. He calls you by your NAME. Some of you have been labeled by the streets, by your past, by your family drama, by teachers or bosses who doubted you. But God doesn't see you through those labels. He calls you like He sees you, chosen, purposed, His.

Now here's the real question: how do you react when He calls?

Moses said, *"Here I am."* Isaiah heard the call and said, *"Here I am, send me"* (**Isaiah 6:8**). **Samuel**, just a boy, didn't even recognize God's voice at first but eventually said, *"Speak, Lord, your servant is listening"* (**1 Samuel 3:10**). But not everyone reacted like that. **Jonah** heard the call and ran the other way, straight into a storm and the belly of a fish (**Jonah 1:3**). **Jeremiah** said he was too young (**Jeremiah 1:6**). **Gideon** said he was too weak (**Judges 6:15**). Different people, different excuses, same God.

So let me ask you, when God tugs on your heart, what's your posture? Do you say, "Nah, not me"? Do you hide like Adam in the garden (**Genesis 3:8-10**)? Do you run like Jonah? Or do you throw your hands up like Isaiah and say, **"Here I am"**?

Here's the thing about being called, it ain't always glamorous. Sometimes it feels heavy. God's call isn't an invitation to a comfy church seat or a chill Sunday routine. It's an assignment. And real assignments come with real weight. To be called is to be entrusted with people, with influence, with responsibility. It means God trusts you to carry something bigger than yourself.

Jesus even said in **Matthew 22:14,** *"Many are called, but few are chosen."* That's not just a fancy line. It means lots of people will hear God's call, but only a few will actually pick up and walk it out. Why? Because calling requires sacrifice. Moses had to leave the palace. Abraham had to leave his home (**Genesis 12:1**). Peter had to drop his nets (**Matthew 4:19-20**). Paul had to give up everything he thought he knew (**Philippians 3:7-8**).

After I responded to God telling me to "go get my family back", I packed up my belongings, said my goodbyes to all my San Diego people and moved up to Modesto out of obedience. I wasn't happy about leaving the city I love, all my connections, my family, my resources, my scene. I deleted about two thousand social media "friends", unfollowed so many connections, and deleted contacts that shouldn't have been on my contact list to begin with. There were things that I needed to release, let go of, and take off just like when Moses was asked to take his sandals off. What are you willing to sacrifice?

When God calls you, He expects obedience. That's it. You might not feel ready, you might feel unqualified, you might be scared, but He'll equip you as you move. You don't need the full plan, you just need to answer. And peep this, make sure your heart is right when moving towards the bush and answering the call. Check the posture of your heart when accepting your assignment.

Think about those three postures:

- **Face Down** - some fall flat in surrender like Abraham (**Genesis 17:3**) or Moses when the glory of God passed by. That's the posture of humility.
- **Open Heart** - some stand open, like Habakkuk, questioning but still listening (**Habakkuk 2:1**). That's the posture of honesty.

- **Hands Up** - some throw both hands in the air, all in, like Isaiah. That's the posture of surrender and availability. Keep it real, most of you know about putting your hands up to surrender right?

Where you at? For some of you, your calling might not look churchy. Maybe God is calling you to start a business that creates jobs. Maybe He's calling you to mentor the younger dudes on your block or inside your pod. Maybe He's calling you to step up as a father, husband, wife, or leader at home. Your calling could be in the streets, the boardroom, the pulpit, or behind prison walls. But don't miss this, you ARE called.

And here's the kicker, your calling usually sits right where your pain and passion collide. Moses was drawn out of the water as a baby and later God used him to draw a whole nation out of Egypt. David fought lions and bears in private before he ever fought Goliath. Paul, who once hunted Christians, became the one leading them. The very area that hurt you the most may become the exact place God uses you.

So let me push this question on you: what's your burning bush? What is God putting in front of you to get your attention? A tragedy, a health scare, a closed door, a divine opportunity? Are you paying attention, or are you ignoring it?

Because the real question isn't "Am I called?" The real question is "Will I answer?"

Handle That

Stop running. If you've been hearing God tug at your heart, even if it scares you or you don't fully understand it, stop ignoring it. Today, make a choice to say, "Here I am." Write it down. Say it out loud. Own it.

Take Note

- When's the last time you felt God tugging at you, even when it didn't make sense?
- Which posture describes you right now, face down, open heart, or hands up?
- What's one thing you know God's been nudging you to do but you've been holding back?

Take It to God

Father, thank You for calling me by name. You didn't call me by my past, my record, or my mistakes. You called me by who You created me to be. Forgive me for the times I've ignored You or run from the call. Give me courage to answer, "Here I am," even when I feel unqualified or afraid. Teach me to trust that if You called me, You'll equip me. Don't let me miss my burning bush moments. In **Jesus' Name, Amen**.

Take Your Sandals Off

"Do not come any closer," the Lord warned. "Take off your sandals, for you are standing on holy ground." - (Exodus 3:5 NLT)

Life and Leadership Lesson

Moses is out there doing the same thing he does every day, just another shift with sheep. Nothing flashy, no spotlight, no followers. Then BOOM! He sees that bush on fire but not burning. He steps closer, curious, and God hits him with something unexpected, "Take off your sandals, this is holy ground."

That move right there is deep. God was saying, "Before you step into My presence, you gotta remove something. You can't come in here the same way you walked around in the desert. Strip it off. Respect My space."

Now pause. Let's make this personal. What is God asking you to take off before you step into His presence? For some it's pride. For others, it's bitterness. Maybe it's guilt over the past, maybe it's the fake persona you carry so people don't see the real you.

For me, I had to take off the idea that I needed credit, clout, or recognition to feel valuable. I had to let go of unforgiveness, pride, lust, shame, guilt, and insecurity. There was so much unforgiveness that I was holding on to that I need to learn to forgive others, ask for forgiveness and learn to forgive myself. I had to remove that because it was weighing me down so heavily. The moment I did was such a relief! Those were my "sandals."

Leaders, creatives, hustlers, inmates, lonely pastors, CEOs, this applies to all of us. Before God can trust you with His assignment, He will check what you're willing to remove.

Think about this: Joshua had to take off his sandals too in **Joshua 5:15** when he encountered the commander of the Lord's army. Same instruction: "Take off your sandals, this is holy ground." Why sandals? Because sandals carried the dirt, the mess, the dust of where you've been. God is saying, "Leave that outside. Don't bring your dirt into My presence."

What about you? Are you willing to take off the stuff you've been carrying so you can walk into what God has for you?

Look at Isaiah. In **Isaiah 6**, when he saw the Lord, he cried out, "Woe to me! I am ruined! For I am a man of unclean lips." And what did God do? He removed the uncleanness, the angel touched his lips with a burning coal. Something had to be stripped away before Isaiah could say, "Here I am, send me."

Or Gideon. Before God used him, He told him to tear down his father's altar to Baal (**Judges 6:25-26**). Again, something had to go before God could bring the victory.

Yup, even Paul, before he became Paul, had to lose his "Saul" identity. He lost his sight, his reputation, and his old name. God stripped him before He used him.

So let me ask you, what's your sandal? What dirt is God asking you to drop at the door before He calls you deeper? Is it ego? Addiction? Fear? Secret sin? Unforgiveness? Comfort?

This ain't just about Moses on a mountain. This is about you, right now, in your cell, your office, your bedroom, or your church. God is saying, "If you want to walk into My presence, if you want to be set apart, if you want to lead My people, take it off."

Leaders, parents, pastors, business owners, real leadership means being stripped before being sent. The world says "add more layers." God says, "strip it down so I can clothe you in My glory."

So here's the lesson, holy ground requires holy surrender. If you want to see God's fire, you gotta let go of what you're holding onto.

Handle That

- Write down one thing God may be asking you to "take off" right now. Don't sugarcoat it.
- Pray over it and make a move this week to actually drop it.
- Every time you walk barefoot somewhere, let it remind you: "I can't carry dirt into His presence."

Take Note

- What are the "sandals" God is asking you to remove before stepping into His call?
- What dirt have you been tracking into holy spaces that God wants you to leave outside?

- How would your leadership look different if you walked into God's presence lighter and stripped of baggage?

Take It to God

Father, thank You for inviting me onto holy ground. Forgive me for the dirt I've tried to bring into Your presence. Show me what You're asking me to take off, and give me the courage to drop it. Teach me that leadership starts with surrender. I don't want to cling to what's comfortable if it keeps me from You. Today, I take off my sandals, I drop my dirt, and I step into Your presence as I am. Use me, shape me, and send me. In **Jesus' Name, Amen.**

The Excuses We Give - (Exodus 3-4)

Life and Leadership Lesson

If you think you've come up with some creative excuses to dodge what God's calling you to do, relax, Moses already beat you to it. At the burning bush, God gave him the clearest assignment in the world: *"Go to Pharaoh, bring My people out."* And instead of saying "Bet, let's roll," Moses hit Him with five excuses. Five. Straight up arguing with God, like God had the wrong dude.

Sound familiar? Well, let's walk through his excuses and see if they sound like any of yours.

Excuse #1: "Who am I?" *(Exodus 3:11)* Moses' first excuse was about his identity. "I'm a nobody. I'm not qualified. I can't do this." We say the same: *"Who am I to lead? Who am I to start this? Who am I to think I could change anything?"* But God's answer was, "It's not about who you are, it's about who *I* am."

Excuse #2: "What if they don't believe me?" *(Exodus 4:1)* Moses worried about people not taking him seriously. You've said it too: *"What if they clown me? What if they don't respect me? What if my past disqualifies me?"* God's answer? He gave Moses signs and power. That means, your credibility doesn't come from people, it comes from God backing you.

Excuse #3: "I'm not a good speaker." *(Exodus 4:10)* Moses stuttered, struggled with words. He thought he needed charisma to lead. How many times have you told God, *"I don't have the skills. I don't talk like that. I'm not educated enough. I'm not polished enough."* But God said, "Who gave man his mouth?" In other words: if I made you, I can use you.

Excuse #4: "I'm not qualified." *(Exodus 3:13)* Moses said, "What if they ask who sent me? I don't have the credentials." That's like us saying, *"I don't have the degree, I don't have the connections, I don't have the paperwork."* God said, "Tell them I AM sent you." The name of God was his credential. And if you belong to Him, it's yours too.

Excuse #5: "Send someone else." *(Exodus 4:13)* This was the last one. Moses just flat out said, "Nah God, I don't want it. Pick someone else." How many times have you done that? God put something in your heart and you dodged it because it felt too heavy, too scary, too risky.

Here's the thing: excuses might feel safe in the moment, but they'll rob you of your purpose. Leadership ain't about being flawless, it's about saying yes when everything in you wants to say no. God already knows your weaknesses. He already knows your insecurities. But He still called you.

So what excuses are you giving God right now? "I'm too old"? "I'm too young"? "I've got too much of a past"? "I don't have the resources"? "I don't feel ready"?

Let me flip it, what if the very thing you think disqualifies you is the exact thing God wants to use?

Handle That

Write down your top three excuses for why you think you can't step into your purpose. Then, next to each one, write what God says about it. Replace your "I can't" with His "I will."

Take Note

- Which one of Moses' excuses sounds the most like yours?
- When you think about stepping into *unlikely leadership*, what's the biggest lie you tell yourself?
- What would change if you stopped dodging the call and just trusted God to fill in the gaps?

Take It to God

Father, I admit I've been making excuses. Just like Moses, I've told You I'm not good enough, not ready, not qualified. I've worried about what people think. I've even asked You to pick someone else. Forgive me for running from what You're calling me to do. Give me courage to stop hiding behind excuses and start walking in faith. Remind me that You don't call the qualified, You qualify the called. I'm tired of stalling. Today I say yes. **In Jesus' Name, Amen.**

What Is Your Burning Bush?

"There the angel of the Lord appeared to him in flames of fire from within a bush. Moses saw that though the bush was on fire it did not burn up." - (Exodus 3:2 NIV)

Life and Leadership Lesson

Moses was just out there doing his normal routine. Same desert, same sheep, same boring grind. Then out of nowhere, BOOM! A bush catches fire but doesn't burn up. That's crazy. God broke His silence in the middle of nowhere, through something Moses couldn't ignore. And here's the key, Moses had to turn aside and pay attention.

Now let's talk about you. What's your burning bush?

God still lights fires today to get our attention. Sometimes it's loud. Sometimes it's subtle. It could be a death in the family that makes you rethink your life. A tragedy that shakes you to your core. A medical diagnosis that reminds you how fragile you are. A breakup that exposes the idol you made out of someone. A layoff that forces you to trust Him instead of your paycheck. A court case hanging over you that can change your life. Shoot, the Bible even says He used a talking donkey once. God will use anything to get your attention.

The problem is, most of us don't pay attention. We get so caught up in routine, so numb from distractions, that we miss the moment God is trying to break in. That's dangerous, because your burning bush moment isn't just about you having a cool experience, it's God pulling you into your purpose.

For those of you who feel like you don't have a calling yet, like you don't even know your "why," let me tell you something: your burning bush is coming. And if you look closely, maybe it's already here. Don't wait for lightning to crack the sky. Pay attention to the small fires God lights in your everyday life. The question is, are you sensitive enough to notice?

Moses' life flipped on that day because he turned to look. If he walked past it, maybe we wouldn't even be reading his story right now. That's the power of paying attention.

So let me ask you: what's God trying to show you? Has He been tugging at your heart through pain? Through silence? Through opportunities you've been too scared to grab? Through people He put in your life to speak truth? Or are you so distracted that you keep walking past your burning bush? Keep an eye out for that calling and chase your purpose.

Handle That

Don't ignore the fire. Write down one situation in your life right now that you think God might be using to get your attention. Then pray over it, asking Him to show you what He's trying to say.

Take Note

- What's one moment in your past where God used pain, tragedy, or change to wake you up?
- Where in your life right now do you sense God trying to get your attention?
- Are you willing to stop, turn aside, and pay attention like Moses did?

Take It to God

Father, open my eyes to see the burning bushes You place in front of me. Help me not to walk past the moments where You're trying to get my attention. Teach me to pay attention to Your voice in the middle of ordinary life. Whether it's through pain, change, or opportunity, I want to recognize it's You speaking. Break through my distractions and my stubbornness. Give me a sensitive spirit to notice the fire and the courage to step closer when You call. **In Jesus' Name, Amen.**

Chapter 7

Age Ain't Nothing But a Number

"Moses was eighty years old, and Aaron was eighty-three when they made their demands to Pharaoh." - (Exodus 7:7 NLT)

Life and Leadership Lesson

As we try to find excuses to NOT do that thing that God is asking of us, we try to hang on to our age as our excuse. Moses was eighty when God called him to confront Pharaoh and lead the Israelites out of Egypt. Most of us think about retiring at that age, slowing down, maybe kicking back with grandkids or just surviving off Social Security. But nah, God said, "Moses, get up, I got work for you."

Let's be real. How many times do we put limits on ourselves because of age? Maybe you think you're too old to start over. Maybe you're young and you think you don't have the experience yet. But the Bible is full of stories showing us that age ain't nothing but a number when God's hand is on your life.

- **Abraham and Sarah** - he was one hundred when he had Isaac. Sarah was ninety when she gave birth. Crazy! You know that had to be God. In **Genesis 18:10-14,** Sarah laughed when she heard she'd have a baby in her old age. Sometimes what you laugh at in disbelief becomes your biggest testimony. God's promises don't have an expiration date.

- **Caleb**, at eighty-five, was still saying, **"Give me this mountain" (Joshua 14:10-12).** He wasn't asking for retirement, he was asking for his next fight. "I am eighty-five years old today, and I'm still as strong now as I was when Moses sent me out." For some of us more mature folks, we're like, "Don't let the gray hair fool you." Faith and fight don't age out.

- **Samuel** was just a little boy when he heard God's voice in the temple (**1 Samuel 3:1-10**).

- **David** was still a teen when he killed Goliath.

- **Timothy** was a young leader when Paul reminded him, **"Don't let anyone look down on you because you are young" (1 Timothy 4:12).** Paul told Timothy, don't wait until you're older to act like a leader. Set the tone *now.*

Yo! See the pattern? God doesn't clock you in and out based on age. He looks at your heart, your willingness, your faith, your desire to do kingdom work. These things make you an *unlikely leader.*

Let me ask you something: have you been disqualifying yourself because you think you're too young or too old? Maybe you're sitting in a cell right now saying, "It's too late for me, my time's passed." Or maybe you're a business owner thinking, "I missed my window." Let me tell you, nah. If Moses could get started at eighty, you can get started right now. Moses was 80 years old when he spoke to Pharaoh. At 80, most people are trying to retire, Moses was just getting started. God don't care how long you've been sitting in the desert, if He says "Go," age don't matter.

Think about this, some of the most dangerous lies the enemy throws at us are about time. "You're too late." "You missed it." "You're too old." Or even, "You're too young, no one will respect you." But God says, "I decide when your time is." **Ecclesiastes 3:1** says *"there's a season for everything under heaven."* That means God has a set time for you to step into your assignment.

Too Young to Lead?

Whenever you use the excuse that you're too young, think about this. **Jeremiah 1:6-7 (NLT)** *"O Sovereign Lord," I said, "I can't speak for you! I'm too young!" The Lord replied, "Don't say, 'I'm too young,' for you must go wherever I send you and say whatever I tell you."* Jeremiah thought his age disqualified him, but God said "nah, I decide when you're ready."

Check this out, **Luke 2:46-47** tells us Jesus was at the temple at twelve years old and was in deep discussion with teachers and they were amazed at his understanding and answers. Dude, preteen Jesus was blowing minds at the temple, what were we doing at twelve years old? You don't even wanna know what we were doing on our block!

Let's talk about David the shepherd boy. In **1 Samuel 16:11-13** The prophet Samuel anointed David king while he was still out watching sheep. This kid was overlooked. You ever feel overlooked? Peep this, David's own family didn't even call him in the room when Samuel came looking for a king. Sometimes people overlook you 'cause they think you're too young or too small, but God's hand finds you where you are. Don't even trip.

Don't forget in **John 6:9-13, The Boy with the Five Loaves and Two Fish.** A kid showed up with a small lunch, and Jesus used it to feed thousands. Don't ever think you're too young or too small to make a big impact when it's in God's hands. Whenever you use the excuse that you're too young, think about this. **Jeremiah 1:6-7 (NLT)** *"O Sovereign Lord," I said, "I can't speak for you! I'm too young!" The Lord replied, "Don't say, 'I'm too young,' for you must go wherever I send you and say whatever I tell you."* Jeremiah thought his age disqualified him, but God said "nah, I decide when you're ready."

Some young cats walk in more wisdom than folks twice their age because they listen to God, not their feelings. I know a young man named Jordan Lunderville that is 22 years old and has been doing ministry since he was 15, starting a bible club at his school, studying the Bible, learning to preach and teaching others. He didn't think he was too young, he ran towards his calling.

Don't let a birth certificate stop your calling. Don't let a calendar tell you when God can or can't use you. Don't let the wrinkles, the grey hairs, or the inexperience talk you out of it. If God said it, then boom, it's your time, no matter what the number says. I'll be 52 years old by the time this book comes out and I feel like I got so many more projects I gotta release in my older years.

My boss, Morris Cerullo was still out teaching God's word at the age of 89 right before he passed away. Age never mattered to them, it shouldn't matter to you either. Purpose has no retirement. If you're still breathing, you're still called, handle it!

Handle That

Ask yourself:

- Have I been saying "I'm too old" or "I'm too young" as an excuse not to move?
- What dream or calling have I put on pause because I think my age disqualifies me?
- What would happen if I stopped looking at the number and just said yes to God right now?

Take Note

Write down the excuses you've made about your age. Then write out how God could flip that and use it for His glory. Example: "I'm too old to learn something new" becomes "I have wisdom and experience that others don't." Or "I'm too young to be taken seriously" becomes "I have passion, energy, and fresh vision."

Take It to God

Father, thank You that my age doesn't limit my calling. Help me to stop putting myself on the bench when You've called me to the game. Show me how to use my years, whether many or few, for Your glory. Give me the courage of Caleb, the faith of Abraham, the boldness of David, and the obedience of Moses. Remind me daily that my time is in Your hands, not mine. **In Jesus' Name, Amen.**

Chapter 8

God Can Even Use That Guy?

"But Moses pleaded with the Lord, 'O Lord, I'm not very good with words. I never have been, and I'm not now, even though you have spoken to me. I get tongue-tied, and my words get tangled.' Then the Lord asked Moses, 'Who makes a person's mouth? Who decides whether people speak or do not speak, hear or do not hear, see or do not see? Is it not I, the Lord? Now go! I will be with you as you speak, and I will instruct you in what to say."
- (Exodus 4:10-12 NLT)

"Instead, God chose things the world considers foolish in order to shame those who think they are wise. And he chose things that are powerless to shame those who are powerful. God chose things despised by the world, things counted as nothing at all, and used them to bring to nothing what the world considers important. As a result, no one can ever boast in the presence of God." - (1 Corinthians 1:27-29 NLT)

Life and Leadership Lesson

This right here is for those *unlikely leaders* who look in the mirror and think, "Nah, God would never use me." Moses tried that. He told God he could not talk right. He brought up his weakness like it was new information. God answered, "I made your mouth. Go." The question is, "Did God call me, and will I move when He says move?"

Let's keep it one hundred. What label have you been wearing that keeps you sitting down when God is telling you to stand up. Ex-con. Dropout. Failure. Addict. Angry. Broke. Too old. Too young. Unpolished. Not churchy enough. Too street. Too corporate. You feel me? God is not confused about your past or your personality. The college degrees you may or may not have. He chose you knowing all of it. And what if God is saying, "You're exactly who I want. I'm going to use that story, that pain, that past, for something bigger"?

The Bible stays showing us how God runs with the unlikely.

- **Gideon** said he was the weakest in the weakest family. God called him a mighty warrior and used him anyway. **Judges 6.**
- **David** was the overlooked little brother in the back with the sheep. God crowned him king. **1 Samuel 16.**
- **Rahab** was a prostitute who hid the spies and ended up in the family line of Jesus. **Joshua 2 and Matthew 1.Peter** denied Jesus three times, then preached and three thousand got saved. **John 21 and Acts 2.**
- **Paul** hunted Christians, then wrote letters that disciple the world. **Acts 9 and 1 Timothy 1:12–16.**
- **The Samaritan woman** had a messy history, but she ran back and brought her whole town to Jesus. **John 4.**
- **The man with a legion of demons** was set free and sent to tell everybody what God had done. **Mark 5.**

- **Jeremiah** said he was too young. **Isaiah** said his lips were unclean. God touched both and sent them. **Jeremiah 1:6-9 and Isaiah 6:5-8**.

You see the pattern? The encounter, the excuse, then the assignment. God does not wait until you feel ready. He meets you as you are and grows you as you go. Availability beats ability. Obedience beats eloquence. The anointing covers the gaps that talent can't cover.

Let's talk like family.

- For the **Inmate** reading this that thinks your record cancels you. My boy, What if your testimony becomes the key that unlocks hope for the next man on the tier?
- **CEO or small business owner**, you feel unqualified because the last venture failed. What if the failure was meant to be a lesson?
- **Creative or influencer**, you think you are not "churchy" enough. What if your lane is exactly where God wants a witness.
- **Pastor or ministry leader**, you keep replaying your worst moment. What if God is trying to turn that scar into a sermon that heals people who would never listen to a perfect life.

God rarely chooses the one who looks most impressive. He chooses the *unlikely* one who will depend on Him the most. **Acts 4:13** says *"the leaders could tell Peter and John were ordinary and untrained, but they recognized one thing. They had been with Jesus"*. That's that glow. That is the difference. Not polish. Just presence.

See, at the bush, Moses didn't believe in himself. He literally said, *"God, You got the wrong guy. I can't even talk right."* And God looked at him like, *"Who do you think made your mouth? If I say you're the one, you're the one."* God did not give him a TED Talk. God gave him a promise. Instead, He says" Bring

Me your weakness and watch Me use it". Some scholars say Moses had a stutter, but your stutter can become a tool that He uses. Your mistakes can become a roadmap for somebody else to find freedom. Stop hiding what God wants to use.

I know I've said, "Send someone else." Sometimes we are quick to say, "that other guy is more qualified." But think about **David taking bread and cheese** to his brothers. If he had said, "Send somebody else," he would have missed Goliath. Small assignments open big doors. Faithfulness in hidden places sets you up for visible victories.

Now let me press you a little more. Are you waiting for a certain resource before you begin? Are you waiting for people to clap before you move? Are you waiting until you never feel fear? You will lose years like that. Start where you are. Use what you have. Trust who is with you. God told Moses to go back to Egypt with the same staff he used to herd sheep. The tool was simple, but God made it powerful.

I've dealt with insecurities my entire life, I'm still insecure. I sometimes walk into a room thinking, "dang, I'm in over my head on this one, these guys are way smarter, more experienced, speak better, have more resources and finances, I don't stand a chance up in here." Then God shows up and with his favor, shines through me to be able to share ideas, share what God has done through me. As nervous as I still get, and as insecure as I still am, God puts me in rooms I never thought I would be in to show off what he can do with our weakness.

We can't sit still in fear. It's about moving while you're afraid because God said "go". **Joshua 1:9**. Leadership is not about never failing. **Proverbs 24:16**. Leadership is not about flexing your strengths It's about stewarding your weaknesses so God gets the glory. **2 Corinthians 12:9.**

So yeah, God can even use "that guy." The wild homie who used to run the block. The single mom who holds it down and thinks nobody sees her. The entrepreneur with two bankruptcies and one more idea. The pastor who almost quit. He can and He will, if you will say yes.

Here's the thing, God specializes in using "that guy", the one everybody else counted out, the one nobody believed in, the one with the rap sheet, the scars, the failures, the addictions. Like my boy Jason Page always says, God uses *the most unlikely*, and that's where I realized that's me, that's us, we are the *"unlikely"* that God uses. We are the *'Unlikely Leaders"*.

Think about it. Moses was a murderer before he ever became a deliverer. David? An adulterer who had blood on his hands. Rahab? A prostitute who ended up in the lineage of Jesus. Peter? The one who denied Jesus three times and still became the rock of the church. Paul? A dude who literally hunted Christians before writing most of the New Testament.

Bro, stop disqualifying yourself. Stop letting shame whisper that you can't be used because you're too far gone. You're not. God is still in the business of choosing the *unlikely*. If He used all those people, why not you?

Maaaan! I fought that far too long. I felt ashamed because of an abuse that I experienced as a youngster. I felt unqualified and unworthy because I'm not very educated. I always hid the fact that I dealt with dyslexia and never told anyone what I was dealing with. I never thought God would use me or someone like me to help others, but God uses the foolish, and that's *ME*!

You see the pattern?

Let me bring it in closer. No one expected my childhood friend Paco Mansin, the wildest dude we knew, to be the guy changing lives in AA meetings, spreading hope, inspiration, and sobriety all over Southern California. That's God's flex. He takes the one you'd never expect and says, *"Watch this."*

It's time to stop sitting on the sidelines thinking, *"Somebody else will do it."* It's time to step into the role God already had in mind for you. The world is waiting on the story only you can tell, the impact only you can make.

Handle That

Write down three things you've believed disqualify you from being used by God. Now flip that question, ask yourself, "How could God use these very things to help somebody else?"

- Write your top three excuses on paper. Cross each one out and write this across the page: "God is with me."
- Pick one small act of obedience you will do in the next 48 hours. Make the call. Enroll in the class. Apologize. Share your testimony with one person. File the paperwork. Start the meeting with two people if that is all you have. Do that dang thing!
- Block one hour this week as a "go" hour. No overthinking. Only actions that match what God already told you.

Take Note

- What labels have people put on you that made you feel "too far gone"?
- Whose life could change if you stopped hiding your story and started using it?
- What would it look like for you to fully say yes to God using you, flaws and all?
- Where have I confused humility with hiding?

- Who is one person I am uniquely positioned to reach because of my story?
- What weakness have I refused to surrender that God keeps pointing at.
- If God gets the glory either way, what am I afraid of losing?
- What excuse have I repeated so long it started sounding like truth?

Take It to God

Father, thank You that You use the most unlikely. Thank You that my past doesn't disqualify me from my future. Forgive me for all the times I believed I was too far gone. Remind me that You can use even my mistakes, my scars, and my struggles for Your glory. Give me the courage to stop disqualifying myself and to step into what You've called me to do. I hear You. I have been stalling, making excuses, and replaying my past like it is stronger than Your promise. Today I give You my weaknesses, my record, my fear, and my doubt and my excuses. Use my life to reach people I could never reach on my own. Make me bold and keep me humble so all the glory goes to You. I say yes. **In Jesus' Name, Amen.**

Chapter 9

What's Your Pharaoh?

"Afterward Moses and Aaron went to Pharaoh and said, 'This is what the Lord, the God of Israel, says: Let my people go, so that they may hold a festival to me in the wilderness."
- (Exodus 5:1 NIV)

Life and Leadership Lesson

When God called Moses, the assignment may have seemed easy, just walk back into Egypt and confront Pharaoh, the most powerful man in the world at that time. The same dude Moses ran from. The same system that wanted him dead.

That's wild. God basically told him, "Go back and face the very thing you've been avoiding."

We all have a Pharaoh, what's yours?

Your Pharaoh may be that thing that's been paralyzing you and making you feel like you'll never break free? Is it fear of failure? Fear of success? Fear of people finding out about your past? Fear of letting your family down? Fear and faith cannot coexist, it's a lie from the enemy. Thats where we always go wrong, when we focus on what can go wrong instead of who is in control.

For my people in recovery, maybe your Pharaoh is your addiction that won't let go. Or that shame that whispers "you'll never be enough". Or maybe it's that pride that keeps you fronting like you're good when you're drowning inside.

For some of you in business, your Pharaoh is that voice saying, *"Don't take the risk. Play it safe."* For those creatives, your Pharaoh says, *"Nobody cares about your art. Nobody will support your vision. Why even try?"* For the leaders, that Pharaoh could be the fear of people turning on you. And for those locked up, your Pharaoh can be that inner voice that says, *"This is all you'll ever be. You'll never change."*

See, Pharaoh doesn't always look like a king in a palace. Sometimes Pharaoh looks like fear and insecurity living rent-free in your head.

Moses didn't stroll into Pharaoh's crib with an army. He walked in with a staff and a word from God. Same with you. You might feel unarmed, but you're not. You've got God's authority. You've got a calling. You've got God on your side. That's all you've ever needed.

So what are you running from that God is telling you to face? And are you gonna keep letting fear paralyze you, or are you finally gonna stand up and say, "Let me go"?

Fear ain't just a feeling, it's a spirit. And it will control you if you let it. But God didn't give you a spirit of fear. He gave you power, love, and a sound mind. Leaders can't lead if they're chained up by fear. Entrepreneurs can't innovate if they're scared of failing. Creatives can't create if they're scared of critics. And nobody can walk in freedom if they keep bowing to Pharaoh.

So here's the challenge: stop letting Pharaoh run your life. It's time to confront what's been holding you back. No more living in fear. Live out your purpose. Confront that fear.

Handle That

Write down the Pharaoh in your life, the fear, the addiction, the shame, the obstacle. Then write next to it: "LET ME GO." Speak it out loud. Don't just think it. Declare it.

Take Note

- What's the Pharaoh you've been avoiding?
- How has fear been controlling your decisions?
- What would your life look like if you stood up and confronted it instead of hiding?

Take It to God

Father, I know my Pharaoh. I know the fear and the chains I've been letting control me. Today I bring it to You. I don't want to live paralyzed anymore. Give me courage like Moses to face what I've been running from. Remind me that You haven't given me a spirit of fear, but of power, love, and a sound mind. Help me stand up and declare freedom over my life, my family, my calling, and my future. I refuse to bow down to Pharaoh anymore. I trust that You will go with me into the places that scare me the most. **In Jesus' Name, Amen.**

Chapter 10

Keep Showing Up,

Even When It Don't Make Sense

"Then the Lord said to Moses, 'Go, tell Pharaoh king of Egypt to let the Israelites go out of his country.' But Moses said to the Lord, 'If the Israelites will not listen to me, why would Pharaoh listen to me, since I speak with faltering lips?' Now the Lord spoke to Moses and Aaron about the Israelites and Pharaoh king of Egypt, and He commanded them to bring the Israelites out of Egypt." - (Exodus 6:10-13 NIV)

Life and Leadership Lesson

Check this out, you finally step into your calling, do what God tells you, and boom, nothing changes. That was Moses. He told Pharaoh, *"Let my people go."* Instead of freedom, Pharaoh made the Israelites' work harder. The people turned on Moses. He's standing there like, *"God, why even send me? Nobody's listening. This whole mission looks like a flop."*

Ever been there? You try to fix your life, but the more you try, the harder it gets. You try to lead your family, and they roll their eyes. You try to start your business, and the bills stack higher than the sales. You try to walk with God, and all hell breaks loose against you. It don't make sense.

Most people quit when that voice creeps in saying, *"See, you ain't built for this. Just give up. Go back to what you know."*

But here's what God told Moses: ***"Go back to Pharaoh. Tell him again."*** In other words… be persistent, keep showing up. Dang! See, leaders aren't the ones who never feel like quitting. Leaders are the ones who keep pushing even when quitting feels easier.

Think about how many blessings have we missed because we stopped one step too early? How many doors were about to open but we walked away because it "didn't make sense"? What if Moses quit after the first rejection? Israel would've stayed in chains.

I'm talking to you right now, the one ready to give up on your dream, your ministry, your business, your family, even your own self. Don't give up. Keep showing up. You got this!

Keep it pushing, even when your lip's trembling, even when nobody claps, even when the crowd boos, even when it looks like nothing's changing. God ain't asking you to understand it. He's asking you to trust Him and keep moving.

So let me ask you: where in your life are you about to quit? What assignment have you been tempted to abandon because the results don't make sense? What if the breakthrough is just a few steps away? Sometimes we give up too soon on that project, on that person, on that business, on that relationship, on that thing that God has called you to be persistent with. Stay the course family.

Handle That

Think of one area where you feel like quitting right now. Write down why you want to quit. Then next to it, write what would happen if you kept showing up anyway. Commit to one more step forward this week.

Take Note

- Where in your life do you feel like throwing in the towel?
- What's one area you've stopped showing up because it didn't make sense?
- How would things change if you committed to persistence instead of giving up?

Take It to God

Father, I'm tired. There are places in my life where I want to quit because nothing seems to change. But I hear You telling me to keep showing up. Remind me that obedience is more important than results I can see right now. Give me strength to push past discouragement, to trust You when it doesn't make sense, and to never give up. Help me lead with persistence, knowing that You are working even when I don't see it. **In Jesus' Name, Amen.**

Chapter 11
Your Red Sea Miracle

"Then Moses stretched out his hand over the sea, and all that night the Lord drove the sea back with a strong east wind and turned it into dry land." - (Exodus 14:21 ESV)

Life and Leadership Lesson

So, imagine this… You're standing at the edge of the Red Sea. Wind in your face, waves crashing, sand blowing, dust from Pharaoh's army in the air. Behind you? Chariots and soldiers that want to drag you back into chains. In front of you? Nothing but deep water. No bridge or no boat. That's crazy pressure, dude. That's the moment where your palms are sweaty, your knees are weak and your arms are heavy, mom's spaghetti… or whatever it says, and you're like, "Lord, what now?" You got no choice but to start those desperate prayers!

Here's the truth, sometimes God waits until we're pressed against the wall, so we know it's Him and not us. If Moses had found a bridge, or if the people had learned to swim, they would've thought it was their hustle that got them through. But God said, "Nah, I'm gonna split this sea so nobody gets the credit but Me."

I've lived that. When my wife got that diagnosis, man, I was at my own Red Sea. The fear was real, the bills stacked, the questions hit me like waves. I didn't have a plan, no backup. All I had was God. My prayers weren't polished or pretty, they were raw and desperate. "God, I need You. Now. Please." I prayed so much I felt like I was running out of words to tell God.

And I know some of you reading this feel that exact weight. I was at the point where I was praying so much and most of it was getting repetitive. I remember telling my friend that I felt like I was running out of things to tell God! As a matter of fact, I'm in my wife's hospital room at the moment as she does treatment while I'm writing this chapter.

So let me ask you, what's your Red Sea right now? What's that impossible thing you need God to split? Is it a court date? A habit that won't let go? A relationship that's barely breathing? Maybe you just got a diagnosis and feel devastated by the news. Maybe you're sitting in a cell, thinking your life is over. Maybe you're in business and the numbers ain't adding up. Maybe you're in ministry and you feel like nobody's listening. Maybe you're a parent crying over your kid who's gone wild. What's the thing that feels like it's gonna drown you? What's that prayer you whispered through tears when nobody else was watching?

Look, Red Sea prayers are different. They're ugly cries. They're not Instagrammable moments. But those are the prayers God responds to. **Hannah** prayed like that for a child (**1 Samuel 1:10-11**). **Hezekiah** prayed like that when he was told he was about to die, and God gave him 15 more years (**2 Kings 20:1-6**). **Jonah** prayed like that from inside the fish (**Jonah 2:1-2**). Even Jesus prayed like that in Gethsemane, sweating drops of blood, begging for another way but still surrendering to the Father (**Luke 22:44**).

Here's the crazy part. Moses didn't fight the Egyptians. He didn't build boats. He didn't run. He just stretched out his hand. That was obedience. Leadership in that moment wasn't about fighting harder, it was about trusting deeper. Sometimes God don't need your hustle, He needs your faith.

And check this, God didn't split the sea in one second. The verse says ***"all that night the Lord drove the sea back."*** God didn't just snap His fingers and drop them on the other side. He didn't hit fast forward. The Word says, *all night long* He sent an east wind. All night. While Pharaoh was charging, while people panicked, while fear screamed louder than faith, God was already at work. The miracle wasn't instant. We gotta trust the process. That means Moses had to wait, holding out his hand, believing God would come through while nothing looked different yet. That's faith, man. That's what leaders, fathers, business owners, and even inmates need to learn, keep standing even when you don't see the miracle yet.

You catch that? Sometimes your miracle comes overnight, slow, steady, like a wind you can't see but you can feel. Sometimes the sea doesn't move until you stretch out your hand and take the step you're too scared to take. Boom! That's it right there. Don't quit in the "all night" season. Your sea will split when God says so. And it ain't always on *our* timing.

You're gonna have people yelling at you, like the Israelites yelled at Moses, *"Did you bring us out here to die?"* You're gonna have your own thoughts shouting louder than the haters. You might feel stuck in the middle, catching heat from both sides. But leadership looks like this: you stand firm, you raise what God already put in your hand, you cry out to Him, and when He says move, you start steppin'.

Fear may tell you to go back. Pride will tell you to fake it. Shame will tell you to sit down. But faith? Faith says, "Lift up your hand, step forward, and watch God do His thing."

David had his Red Sea moment when he faced Goliath with nothing but a sling (**1 Samuel 17**). Daniel had his when he stood in that lion's den (**Daniel 6**). Paul and Silas had theirs in prison when they sang at midnight and God shook the ground (**Acts 16:25-26**). And Jesus Himself had the cross, the ultimate Red Sea moment where death was in front of Him and the enemy breathing down His neck. But because He pushed through, He split eternity wide open for us.

So, what if God is already sending the wind, but you just can't see it yet? What if your job isn't to fix the sea, but to stretch out your hand, take the step, and trust the One who parts it?

Don't trip. The same God that split the Red Sea for Moses can split your situation too. He doesn't always move instantly, but He always moves faithfully.

Handle That

Write down your Red Sea moment right now. Be real with it. Don't sugarcoat it. Then every day this week, take it before God in prayer. Don't pray soft prayers. Pray desperate ones. Write it down, pray it out loud, believe it like your life depends on it.

- Name your Red Sea out loud. No fluff. "God, my Red Sea is _______."
- Write down one step of obedience you can take while you wait. Make the call. Send the text. Apologize. Enroll. Ask for help. Do whatever that thing may be.
- Pray tonight and thank God as if the wind is already blowing.

Take Note

- What enemy is chasing you right now, and what sea is blocking you?
- What fear do you need to surrender so you can take the next step?

- How do I usually pray when I'm desperate, do I cry out or do I shut down?
- Am I trying to fix things myself instead of stretching out my hand and trusting God?
- Do I believe God can still part seas in my life today?

Take It to God

Father, You see my Red Sea. You see what's chasing me and what's blocking me. I feel trapped, and I need You to make a way where there is no way. Blow Your wind over my situation. Drive back what's trying to drown me. Just like You split the sea for Moses, split the sea in my life. Teach me to stand, to raise what You put in my hand, and to step when You say step. Teach me to pray desperate prayers, to stand in faith even when I don't see it yet, and to trust You with my life. Turn this sea into a road and let people see Your glory in my life. Thank You that You're still the God of miracles, and I'm trusting You to show up in my story. **In Jesus' Name, Amen.**

Just Stand Still

"But Moses told the people, 'Don't be afraid. Just stand still and watch the Lord rescue you today. The Egyptians you see today will never be seen again."
- (Exodus 14:13 NLT)

Life and Leadership Lesson

Moses and the people are standing at the edge of the Red Sea, it's chaos. People screaming, kids crying, soldiers shouting. Everybody's panicking, pointing fingers at Moses, "You brought us out here to die!" That's pressure.

And what does Moses say? *"Stand still. Don't be afraid. Watch what God's about to do."*

That's wild because everything in us screams the opposite. When chaos hits, we want to do something. But here God was saying, "Nah. Chill. Stand still and let Me handle it."

See, this leadership thing isn't *just* about action. It's about discernment. Knowing when to stop and when to take off. Knowing when God is saying, "Move" and when He's saying, "Be still." Sometimes the hardest leadership move is to not move, because *that* takes trust. The lesson here is this: **stillness is not weakness. Stillness is strength. Stillness is surrender.** Because when you stand still, you're declaring, "God, I trust You more than my panic. I believe You got this even when I don't see the way."

Joseph had to stand still in a prison cell before he even saw the palace. Waiting ain't wasted. Think about Jehoshaphat in **2 Chronicles 20:17. Surrounded by armies, the word of the Lord came and said,** *"But you will not even need to fight. Take your positions; then stand still and watch the Lord's victory."* Same thing. God wanted them to stand firm, not scramble.

Or think of David, he had to stand still in caves for a hot minute before becoming a king. And in **Psalm 27:14**: *"Wait patiently for the Lord. Be brave and courageous. Yes, wait patiently for the Lord."* That's not weak waiting, that's active trust. Patience is a muscle.

And don't forget Jesus. In **Mark 4:39** He's asleep in the boat while His disciples are losing their minds in the storm. They're freaking out, He's at peace. Why? Because He knew His Father had it covered. Even Jesus waited thirty years before He stepped into ministry. That's what leadership looks like under pressure.

So let me flip this to you:

- What's your Red Sea moment right now? Is it your bills stacking up? A diagnosis that wrecked you? Sitting in a cell with no clear path forward?
- Do you panic and try to force things, or do you stand still and let God do what only He can do?
- What's harder for you, moving fast or waiting on God's timing?

For some of you, sometimes survival mode keeps you reacting fast to everything. But not every fight is yours. For those in business, sometimes you're so used to fixing things you won't stop long enough to see God's rescue. For those in ministry, sometimes you're burnt out trying to fight battles God never told you to fight. For those leading a family, don't wait till it's too late to start leading your spouse and kids in the ways of the Lord because the world is waiting to lead them in another direction. Trust me on this one.

Let's keep it real. There have been times in my life where I wanted to force it. Make something happen. But God had to teach me the power of stillness. Sometimes the loudest move you can make is no move at all. The question is, can you trust Him enough to wait?

So let me ask you, where in your life is God saying, "Stand still"? What sea are you staring at while the enemy's breathing down your neck? What fight are you trying to win in your own strength that God is saying, "Let Me handle it"? Stillness is harder than hustle. Anybody can move. But can you be still when everything in you wants to run? That's faith.

Handle That

This week, identify one area where you've been rushing, forcing, or stressing to make something happen. Instead of reacting, stop and pray before you move. Ask God, "Do You want me to stand still here, or step forward?"

Take Note

- What battles am I fighting that God already said He would fight for me?
- Where do I struggle most with standing still?
- How would my leadership look different if I trusted God's timing more than my instincts?
- Where in your life do you feel like you're stuck between the Red Sea and Pharaoh's army?
- How have you been trying to fix it on your own instead of standing still?
- What would it look like to actually wait and watch God move?

Take It to God

Father, You know I don't like waiting. You know I'd rather hustle, push, or force it. But I hear You telling me to stand still. Teach me to trust You when I feel cornered. Show me how to be patient and still without losing faith. Help me lead my family, my business, my ministry, and myself with wisdom instead of panic. Fight the battles I can't fight, and remind me that stillness doesn't mean weakness, it means trusting You. I admit it's hard for me to stand still when everything feels like it's falling apart. I like control. I like action. But You're teaching me that leadership isn't always about doing, it's about trusting. Help me to pause when You say pause, and to move when You say move. Teach me to be still and know that You are God. Calm my heart in the chaos. I trust that You will rescue me, just like You rescued Israel at the Red Sea. **In Jesus' Name, Amen.**

Time for Some Action

"Then the Lord said to Moses, 'Why are you crying out to me? Tell the people to get moving!" - (Exodus 14:15 NLT)

"There is a time for everything, and a season for every activity under the heavens" - (Ecclesiastes 3:1)

"Faith by itself, if it is not accompanied by action, is dead." - (James 2:17)

Life and Leadership Lesson

Boom! That hits hard. Imagine this. Israel is freaking out at the Red Sea, Moses is crying out to God, and God basically says, "Why you still praying? Get moving!" Crazy, right? It's like God is saying, *"Stop praying. Move."*

Think about that. God told Moses to stop praying. Not because prayer wasn't important, but because it wasn't time to keep talking, it was time to start walking. Some of us are experts at talking. We can pray long prayers, take notes, plan, strategize, and have meetings about meetings. But at some point, God is like, *"Enough talk. Let's go."*

Leaders don't just sit in circles and talk about it. Leaders step out. They move when God says move.

For my brothers locked up reading this, maybe you've been telling yourself you'll get serious about your purpose when you get out. Nah. Start now. Pick up that Bible, mentor the young dudes on the tier, work on your discipline, let God shape you in the cell so you're ready when the doors open.

For my entrepreneurs, how many ideas are sitting in your notebook collecting dust? How many "plans" are you pitching to yourself but never launching? God gave you vision, but vision without action is just daydreaming. Faith without works is dead. Boom!

For the believer waiting for a sign, sometimes the sign is the fact that God already spoke. He told Moses, "Tell them to move." The same God who split seas back then is waiting to split something in your life, but He won't do it while you're standing still hiding behind "I'm still praying about it.

There is a time when prayer turns into movement. Don't get it twisted, prayer is everything. But there comes a moment when praying has to lead to action. **James 2:17** says it plain, ***"So you see, faith by itself isn't enough. Unless it produces good deeds, it is dead and useless."***

We've all been there. Sitting on an idea, waiting for the perfect time to launch that business, write that book, step into that ministry, fix that relationship. And God's like, "Enough waiting. Move!" Leaders can't stay frozen in fear or indecision. Leadership requires movement.

So let me ask you, what's paralyzing you? Fear? Doubt? Comfort? Laziness? That inner voice saying, *"I'm not ready yet"*? Because fear will freeze you. Comfort and excuses will keep you stuck and will chain you down just like Egypt did. So ask yourself: what's the thing you've been stalling on? The call you won't make, the forgiveness you won't give, the book you won't start, the business you won't launch, the step of faith you're scared to take? What would shift if you stopped overthinking and just obeyed?

Look at Joshua in **Joshua 1:9**, ***"This is my command, be strong and courageous! Do not be afraid or discouraged. For the Lord your God is with you wherever you go."*** God didn't say sit down, He said go. Or Nehemiah, when he heard Jerusalem's walls were broken, he prayed, yes, but then he got to work. He organized, he built, he moved (**Nehemiah 2:17-18**).

Even Peter in **Matthew 14** had to step out of the boat to walk on water. If he stayed seated, he never would've experienced that miracle. Sometimes miracles are waiting on the other side of movement.

So let me ask you:

- Where in your life are you still crying out when God is telling you to move?
- What dream or vision has God placed in your hand that you're too scared to step into?
- What's paralyzing you right now, fear, doubt, comfort, excuses?

For my brothers inside, maybe God's telling you to stop waiting for the system or people to change your life. Start moving right there in your cell. Build yourself spiritually, mentally, emotionally. For the businessman, maybe it's finally launching that idea or making that tough decision you've been avoiding. For the street leader, maybe it's stepping up and breaking a cycle instead of just talking about it. For the pastor, maybe it's moving forward on that vision God gave you, even if people doubt it.

Leadership ain't just about praying safe prayers. It's about risking it all because God said go. Sometimes the Red Sea doesn't part until you take a step toward it. God already gave you what you need. The staff is in your hand. The sea is in front of you. The enemy is behind you. It's go-time.

Handle That

Pick one thing you've been putting off. Just one. Write it down, then take the first step toward it within the next 24 hours. Call, apply, post, start, build, write, whatever it is. No excuses, no delay. I had to personally put this challenge into action to start and finish this book.

- Write down one area where you've been stuck praying but not moving.
- Take one action step this week that matches your prayer.
- Remind yourself daily: faith is motion.

Take Note

- What fear or excuse has been paralyzing you?
- Where in your life has God already told you to move, but you're still "waiting"?
- What's the one step you know you need to take right now?
- Am I hiding behind prayer because I'm scared to act?

- Where has God already told me to move but I've stalled out?
- What action step today would prove that I trust God's promise?

Take It to God

Father, thank You for hearing my prayers, but also for reminding me that faith requires action. Give me the courage to move when You say move. Open doors that need to be opened and help me to step into the opportunities You've placed in front of me. Teach me to lead by example, not just with words but with bold steps of faith. Thank You for the reminder that faith isn't just words, it's movement. Forgive me for the times I've hid behind prayer when You already told me to act. Give me strength to push past fear, laziness, or comfort and step into the next thing You're calling me to do. Teach me to lead by example, not just talking about faith, but living it out. I trust You to part the waters when I move in obedience. **In Jesus' Name, Amen.**

Chapter 12

Sing in the Wilderness

"Then Moses and the Israelites sang this song to the Lord: 'I will sing to the Lord, for He is highly exalted. Both horse and driver he has hurled into the sea." - (Exodus 15:1 NIV)

Life and Leadership Lesson

There's a whole lot we can learn from the "wilderness season", so if you want a deeper dive into this topic I suggest you check out my buddy, Jordan Lunderville's book called "Don't Waste The Wilderness" for a more extensive study of this subject.

Now, picture this: the Red Sea just split wide open, you walked through walls of water on dry ground, Pharaoh's army is swallowed up behind you, and you're standing in freedom on the other side. What's the first thing Moses and the Israelites do? They don't run to build something, they don't argue about food, they don't even start scouting the next move. Nah, they stop and break out into a song. Right there, in the wilderness. That's the sound of gratitude.

Think about it. These people had been slaves for 400 years, and the first breath of real freedom turns into a praise party. They didn't have much, but they had a song.

Now let me hit you with this… How do you react after God comes through for you? Do you keep it pushing like nothing happened, or do you stop and thank Him? Some of us treat God like an Uber driver, He gets us where we want to go, and we just hop out like, "Cool, thanks," and keep moving. Nah. Real leaders stop and give God glory.

Singing in the wilderness is powerful because it shifts your focus. Instead of stressing about what's ahead, you remind yourself of what He already did. Moses knew the next challenges were coming, food, water, enemies, but first came the song. It's like saying, "God, before I worry about what's next, I'm gonna worship You for what You already did."

And let's keep it real: I'm probably the worst singer you're gonna find, ask my wife. But I'll be singing under my breath or humming a tune along to a song while I'm deep in the middle of going through some madness. Maybe your wilderness right now are prison walls, hospital rooms, financial stress, family drama, the grind of business. Maybe you feel stuck, but that's the perfect time to sing. Not because it feels good, but because it puts your eyes back on God.

Paul and Silas sang while chained in prison, and boom!… doors flew open (**Acts 16:25-26**). David sang in caves when Saul was chasing him down (**Psalm 57**). Praising God in song is like an act of defiance against fear, doubt, and hopelessness.

Leaders, do your people see you worry, or do they see you worship? Are you known for stressing, or are you known for praising? Do you set the tone for your team, your family, your congregation, your homies by how you react when pressure hits? Because leadership ain't just about being organized and having a dope strategy. It's about having a grateful spirit.

Handle That

This week, stop and sing. For real though, I don't care if you sound like Lenny Kravitz, Whitney Houston, Bruno Mars, or a dying cat. Sing a song of gratitude. Blast worship music in your car, hum something in your cell, sing over your business, your family, your crew. Lead your people by being the one who praises even when it don't make sense.

Take Note

- What's one thing God has already done for you that you haven't really thanked Him for?
- Do you treat God's miracles like one-time events, or do you keep them in front of you with worship?
- What's your wilderness right now, and what would it look like to sing right in the middle of it?

Take It to God

Father, thank You for those crazy Red Sea moments in my life. Thank You for pulling me out of situations that should have probably drowned me. Help me not to forget what You've done. Teach me to sing even in the wilderness, when things are uncertain and I don't know what's next. Let my song shift the atmosphere for my family, my business, my community, and even for those who doubt me. Remind me that worship is a weapon and that gratitude is leadership. **In Jesus' Name, Amen.**

Provision in the Wilderness

"Then the LORD said to Moses, "I will rain down bread from heaven for you. The people are to go out each day and gather enough for that day. In this way I will test them and see whether they will follow my instructions." - (Exodus 16:4 NIV)

Life and Leadership Lesson

The wilderness is where you find out who God really is. And his provision in the wilderness tells us that he takes care of us even in that dry season when we feel our lowest.

When the Israelites were out there in the desert, they didn't have Costco, UberEats, or a job to clock into. They had nothing but heat, dust, and hunger. And instead of letting them starve, God dropped **manna** from heaven (**Exodus 16:4**). Fresh bread every morning. Boom. Then when they wanted meat, God sent **quail (Exodus 16:12-13)**. When they were dying of thirst, God told Moses to strike the rock and **water poured out (Exodus 17:6)**. Their **clothes and sandals**? They didn't even wear out for forty years (**Deuteronomy 29:5**). I mean I've had some Chuck Taylor All Stars that lasted a few years but come on, forty years of your gear and your kicks lasting? That's provision right there!

God was showing them, "I got you. Even out here in the wilderness, I got you."

Now let me make it personal. When my wife went through her health challenges and couldn't work, we hit that wilderness. Bills stacked up, finances dropped, and it felt like we were drowning. But somehow, and I know it was God, He kept providing. He sent help, opened doors, and kept us afloat when, on paper, we should've gone under. That's manna. That's quail. That's water from the rock.

So, what's your wilderness story? Was it when you were locked up, and God gave you peace in a cell that made no sense? Was it when you lost a job and somehow your kids still ate every day? Was it when tragedy struck and you thought you couldn't breathe, but God kept your lungs pumping?

Here's the thing, the wilderness can always teach you more than the mountaintop. On the mountaintop, you celebrate. In the wilderness, you learn to trust. And trust is the foundation of leadership.

Moses had to trust God daily. Notice this, manna only lasted for one day. If they tried to store it up, it rotted (**Exodus 16:20**). Why? Because God wanted them to depend on Him every morning, not just once a week. Leaders, that's the same with us. You can't live off yesterday's blessing, yesterday's bread. You gotta wake up and trust Him fresh every day.

David said in **Psalm 37:25**, *"I was young and now I am old, yet I have never seen the righteous forsaken or their children begging bread."* Jesus said in **Matthew 6:11**, *"Give us today our daily bread."* Not monthly bread. Not quarterly bread, Not yearly bread. Daily bread.

That means whether you're running a business, leading a church, holding down your family, or even surviving inside a cell, you're being taught to trust God on new levels every day.

So, if God provided in your wilderness, don't forget Him on your mountaintop. Too many leaders get blessed and then start acting like it was them who did it. Nah, it was Him all along. Don't waste your wilderness lesson.

Handle That

This week, stop and write down three ways God has provided for you in your wilderness, times when you couldn't explain it, but He came through. Then ask yourself: am I leading in a way that reminds people where my provision really came from?

Take Note

- What's the biggest "wilderness" season I've been through?
- How did God provide for me in that time?
- Do I trust Him daily now, or only when I'm desperate?
- Am I teaching others how to trust Him by how I live and lead?

Take It to God

Father, thank You for being my provider in the wilderness. Thank You for manna when I was hungry, water when I was thirsty, and quail when I was tired of the same old thing. Forgive me for the times I forgot that You carried me through when I had nothing. Teach me to trust You daily, not just when I'm in trouble. Help me lead with faith so others can see Your provision through my life. **In Jesus' Name, Amen.**

Chapter 13
Building Your Team

"The Lord said to Moses: 'Bring me seventy of Israel's elders who are known to you as leaders and officials among the people. Have them come to the tent of meeting, that they may stand there with you. I will come down and speak with you there, and I will take some of the power of the Spirit that is on you and put it on them. They will share the burden of the people with you so that you will not have to carry it alone." - (Numbers 11:16-17 NIV)

"But select capable men from all the people, men who fear God, trustworthy men who hate dishonest gain, and appoint them as officials over thousands, hundreds, fifties and tens. Have them serve as judges for the people at all times, but have them bring every difficult case to you; the simple cases they can decide themselves. That will make your load lighter, because they will share it with you. If you do this and God so commands, you will be able to stand the strain, and all these people will go home satisfied." - (Exodus 18:21-23)

Life and Leadership Lesson

Let's keep it real, too many people think leadership is about power, fame, control, influence, or money. But biblical leadership? That's about serving others through humility, and responsibility. Boom. That's wild right? It flips the whole thing upside down.

Moses was leading millions of people through the wilderness. Can you imagine that pressure? Complaints every day, arguments, drama, hunger, fear, and he was trying to carry it all himself. Jethro, his father-in-law, saw him burning out and dropped some wisdom: ***"You can't do this alone. Pick men who fear God, who are trustworthy, who hate corruption, and share the load."***

God later told Moses to bring seventy elders, men already respected by the people, and He put His Spirit on them so they could carry the burden too. That's leadership, not doing it all by yourself, but raising up others who can lead well.

So what are the traits of real leaders?

1. **They Fear God.** That's number one. If someone doesn't respect God, they'll abuse power, and lead selfishly. **Proverbs 9:10** says **"the fear of the Lord is the beginning of wisdom"**. Without that foundation, they're dangerous with influence.
2. **They're Trustworthy.** Not perfect, but consistent. Someone whose word holds weight. **Proverbs 20:7** says **"the righteous man walks in integrity, his children are blessed after him."** If you can't trust them with small things, don't trust them with big things.

3. **They Hate Corruption.** The Bible calls it **"dishonest gain."** Leaders can't be driven by greed or ego. Jesus said in **Matthew 6:24 "you can't serve both God and money."** If their loyalty is for sale, they're not fit to lead.

4. **They Share the Load.** Leaders don't just take power, they take responsibility. They step into the weight of serving others. Jesus Himself said in **Matthew 23:11, "The greatest among you will be your servant."** Leadership is service.

Here's the kicker, Moses didn't look for the loudest, flashiest dude, or most popular people. He looked for the ones already living it out quietly, faithfully, in the background. Real leaders don't chase titles, they chase God.

So, what traits are you showing right now? Are you leading like a servant leader, or are you chasing the spotlight? Are you making decisions based on integrity, or on what benefits you most? Are you carrying the people God gave you, or are you making them carry you?

Whether you're running a church, a business, a construction crew, a band, these traits matter. Who you are off the stage, when nobody's watching, is the real test of leadership.

Handle That

Do a self-check. Write down the four traits: Fear of God, Trustworthiness, Hatred of Corruption, Servanthood. Rate yourself honestly in each one. Where are you strong? Where do you need work? Then pick one area to focus on this week.

Take Note

- Do I fear God enough to lead humbly and wisely?
- Can people really trust my word, my actions, my character?
- Do I privately chase dishonest gain, money, that clout, the influence, or do I hate it like God does?
- Am I serving God's people, or expecting them to serve me?

Take It to God

Father, thank You for showing me what real leadership looks like. Forgive me for the times I've chased titles or power instead of serving people. Teach me to fear You, to walk in integrity, to hate corruption, and to lead as a servant. Raise up others around me with the same traits so we can share the load together. Shape me into the kind of leader You can trust with Your people. **In Jesus' Name, Amen.**

Who's Holding Up Your Arms?

"When Moses' hands grew tired, they took a stone and put it under him and he sat on it. Aaron and Hur held his hands up, one on one side, one on the other, so that his hands remained steady till sunset." - (Exodus 17:12 NIV)

Life and Leadership Lesson

Leadership will expose your limits. Moses found that out real quick. His arms got heavy, and when they dropped, the whole army started losing. Israel didn't win that battle because Moses was strong. They won because Moses had a squad, Aaron and Hur - who held him up when he couldn't hold himself up anymore.

Moses was chosen by God, he carried God's authority, and led the people, but even *he* got tired. His arms dropped and the battle turned against them. See, you can be called and anointed, and still run out of strength.

God didn't expect Moses to do it alone. If Moses needed help, what makes you think you don't? We need those around us that can lovingly call out our crap when we start to slip up. We don't need yes-men, we need those that can protect our blind spots and point out some of the things we don't see ourselves.

Let's be real. Some of us push people away because we want to look strong. We don't want to admit we're tired, we're too prideful to look weak, but sometimes you need to let others lift you.

Scripture tells us:

- Jonathan was that friend for David, encouraging him when Saul wanted to kill him (**1 Samuel 23:16-17**).
- Barnabas was that encourager for Paul, even taking a risk on him when nobody trusted his conversion (**Acts 9:27**).
- Jesus Himself had Peter, James, and John go with Him to Gethsemane when His soul was "sorrowful to death" (**Matthew 26:36–38**). Think about it. Even Jesus leaned on His circle in His hardest moment.

So, whose arms are you holding up? Who in your circle needs you to step in and carry some of their weight? Leadership is not just about who helps you, it's about who you help. Maybe it's your brother behind bars, your co-worker grinding through depression, or your spouse at home carrying more than they can handle. On the flipside, who's holding up your arms? Who's there when you're drained, when the weight of leading gets too heavy? Do you even have people like that, or are you trying to grind it out solo?

My pops also used to say, "Show me who your friends are and I'll tell you who you are." **Proverbs 13:20** backs it up: ***"Whoever walks with the wise becomes wise, but the companion of fools will suffer harm."*** Who you surround yourself with matters. Your crew can determine whether you win battles or take losses. See, your circle matters. And **Proverbs 22:24-25** warns not to hang with people who are hot-tempered or you might learn their ways. **Bad company corrupts good morals (1 Corinthians 15:33)**. The wrong crew could be your entire downfall.

The paralyzed man in **Mark 2** is another powerful example. He couldn't get to Jesus on his own, but his boys carried him, tore the roof open, and lowered him down. Jesus healed him not just because of his faith, but because of *their* faith. Boom! That's the power of a solid crew. That miracle happened because of who he was surrounded by.

So, who's in your circle? Are your people lifting you up or pulling you down? Are they holding your arms like Aaron and Hur, carrying you like the paralyzed man's friends, or are they adding more weight to your load?

This ain't just about who's around you, it's also about who you are to others. Are you carrying anyone to Jesus when they can't carry themselves? Are you the kind of person who points people to God, or the kind who pulls them deeper into madness?

Listen, whether you're a pastor, a business owner, a musician, or an inmate, you're not just picking a crew, you're picking your future. The ones closest to you will shape your decisions, your character, your destiny. Even Jesus rolled with twelve, and I'm sure He prayed before choosing them. He didn't play with His circle, why should you?

Handle That

My pops would say, "there's two types of people around you, those that hurt and those that help, and if they ain't helping you, then they're hurting you!" Do an audit of your circle. Write down the top five people you spend the most time with. Are they building you, carrying you, holding you up, or draining you? Pray over that list, and if God tells you to cut ties, be obedient. Now flip it: write down one person you can lift up this week. Write down the names of the people who hold you up when you're weak. Then write down whose arms you're holding up. If you can't name anybody in either category, it's time to pray and build your team.

Take Note

- Who in my life lifts me up when I'm weary?
- Whose arms am I helping hold up?
- Do I surround myself with people who pull me closer to God or away from Him?
- Am I trying to lead alone when God has blessed me with a team?

Take It to God

Father, thank You for the friends who've carried me, encouraged me, and held me up when I couldn't stand on my own. Show me who in my circle is sent by You and who isn't. Teach me to be the kind of friend who builds faith, not doubt. Help me choose wisely who I walk with, and give me courage to let go of the ones who keep me from You. Thank You for showing me that leadership was never meant to be done alone. Forgive me for the times I've tried to carry everything by myself. Teach me to lean on the Aarons and Hurs You've placed in my life. Help me to be that kind of friend and leader for others too. Build my circle with people of faith, loyalty, and courage. And when I get tired, remind me that I don't have to fake it, I can lean on You and the team You gave me. **In Jesus' Name, Amen.**

Chapter 14

How Do You Use Your Influence?

"So Moses was educated in all the learning of the Egyptians, and possessed great influence through his eloquence and his achievements." - (Acts 7:22 Weymouth New Testament)

Life and Leadership Lesson

Moses wasn't just some random shepherd that God pulled out of nowhere. Before the desert, before the staff, before Pharaoh, Moses grew up in Pharaoh's house. He was educated, trained in leadership, understood that Egyptian wisdom, and the Bible says he was *powerful in speech and action.* That's real influence.

But don't get it twisted, Moses didn't earn that influence on his own. He was supposed to be dead as a baby, but God spared him. He was drawn out of the Nile and was raised and trained in a palace he didn't belong to. Every ounce of that influence was given to him by God. The question was, what was he gonna do with it?

That's the same question I'm throwing at you. What are you doing with your influence? And don't front, you have influence. Influence ain't just about having a blue check or a million followers. Influence is the crew you lead, the kids who watch you, the people at work who copy your habits, the cellmate who listens when you talk, the little cousin who wants to be like you, the church member who looks up to you. Whether you're a CEO, a teacher, a rapper, a foreman on a job site, a band member, or an inmate, somebody is watching.

The Bible is full of people who had influence and had to decide what to do with it. Let's take a look at King Saul, he had influence but misused it, and it was his downfall (**1 Samuel 15**). Look at David: he used his influence to bring glory to God when he fought Goliath, but he also abused it with Bathsheba, and the fallout hit his whole family (**2 Samuel 11**). Look at Solomon: the wisest man alive, but when his influence got corrupted by chasing women and idols, it fractured the nation (**1 Kings 11**).

Influence is the currency of leadership. Influence is heavy. It can build or break, bless or curse. **Proverbs 29:2** says, ***"When the righteous are in authority, the people rejoice; but when the wicked rule, the people groan."*** In other words, your influence ripples. People either rejoice under your leadership or groan under your weight. Which one is it with you?

Jesus Himself talked about it in **Matthew 5:13-16**. He said we're the salt of the earth and the light of the world. Salt preserves and light exposes. That means your influence is supposed to keep things from rotting and help others see. But if you lose your saltiness, you're useless. If you hide your light, you're wasting the influence God gave you.

Let's keep it real. Some of us misuse influence to feed our ego, get money, get clout, get validation. Some of us waste it by sitting on it, never stepping into the role God gave us. Some of us have squandered it, he gave you the platform, and threw it away. And some of us surrender it back to God and let Him multiply it for His glory. Which one are you?

Leaders, hustlers, musicians, church folks, you all got influence. The question is, are you mismanaging it? Are you pointing people to yourself or to Jesus? Are you multiplying life or multiplying destruction?

Handle That

Write down three ways you currently influence people. Then ask yourself: are these ways pushing people closer to God or pulling them further away? Pick one area where you've been misusing your influence and surrender it to God this week.

Take Note

- Who in my life is being shaped by my choices, words, or example right now?
- Am I using my influence to serve or to be served?
- What would it look like if I surrendered all my influence back to God?

Take It to God

Father, thank You for trusting me with influence, even when I didn't deserve it. Forgive me for the times I've wasted it or misused it for myself. Teach me to use every bit of influence You've given me to serve others and point people to You. Keep me humble, keep me accountable, and keep me focused on building Your kingdom, not my own. **In Jesus' Name, Amen.**

Influence the Influencers

"When his father-in-law saw all that Moses was doing for the people, he said, 'What is this you are doing for the people? Why do you alone sit as judge, while all these people stand around you from morning till evening?' ... Moses listened to his father-in-law and did everything he said." - (Exodus 18:14-24 NIV)

Life and Leadership Lesson

You see, Moses is the man in charge. He's the one everyone's looking towards for answers. Millions of people depending on him, and bring him problems. Sun up to sun down, everybody's lined up at his tent. If that was today, Moses would've had people blowing up his phone, his DMs, his email, nonstop. He would be running on fumes.

And then Jethro, his father-in-law, steps in. He's not in the spotlight, he's not the one parting seas or climbing mountains, but he sees what Moses doesn't see. He says, "Yo, what you're doing isn't good. You can't do this alone." Then he gives him a system, shows him how to delegate, and in doing that, saves Moses from burning out and helps Israel move forward.

Boom. That's wild. Jethro influenced the influencer. He didn't need the mic, the title, the credit, or the fame. He just needed wisdom and courage to speak into the leader's life.

Now, let's bring it forward. There was a nurse named **Ethel Kurr**. No platform, no pulpit, no social media following. She worked quietly in an orphanage. But she led a broken little orphan boy named **Morris Cerullo** to Jesus. That boy grew up to become an evangelist who preached the gospel to millions around the world. Today, millions know Morris Cerullo, but very few know Ethel Kurr. Yet without her, none of it happens.

See, that's influence. And here's where most leaders mess up, we confuse fame with impact. We think influence means having the most followers, the biggest stage, the biggest building. But God says it's about faithfulness. **Luke 16:10** says, ***"Whoever can be trusted with very little can also be trusted with much."*** Sometimes your "little" is actually someone else's "much."

Think about it, Andrew in the Gospels ain't as famous as Peter, James, or John. But guess what? Andrew was the one who brought Peter to Jesus (**John 1:40–42**). Without Andrew, there's no Peter preaching on Pentecost, no Peter leading the early church. Andrew wasn't in the spotlight, but he influenced the influencer.

Or look at Barnabas in Acts. His name literally means "son of encouragement." He vouched for Paul when nobody else trusted him (**Acts 9:27**). He took John Mark under his wing when Paul gave up on him (**Acts 15:37-39**). Without Barnabas, Paul doesn't get his shot, and John Mark doesn't come back strong to write the Gospel of Mark.

Boom. You see it yet? Some of the most powerful leaders in history only got there because an *unlikely leader* influenced them quietly behind the scenes.

So let me ask you: are you willing to play that role? Are you okay if God uses you to impact one person instead of millions, knowing that one person might go on to touch millions? Or do you need the spotlight too bad?

The people you influence, and the ones who influence you, shape your destiny. **Proverbs 27:17** says, *"As iron sharpens iron, so one person sharpens another."*

Influence is bigger than followers. Influence is legacy. Are you living in a way that multiplies leaders, or just adds likes to your social media?

Handle That

This week, shift your mindset. Stop asking, "How many people am I leading?" Start asking, "Who am I pouring into?" Find one person you can really invest in. Encourage them, teach them, or just show up for them. Don't worry about credit. Focus on impact.

Take Note

- Who has influenced me the most in my life? Do they even know it?
- Am I too focused on chasing followers instead of investing in the few God gave me?
- If I influenced just one person who went on to change the world, would I be okay with that?

Take It to God

Father, thank You for the people who influenced me, even when nobody else saw it. Forgive me for chasing recognition instead of legacy. Teach me to see the value of pouring into the one, not just chasing the many. Help me be okay with being the Jethro, the Andrew, the Barnabas, the Ethel Kurr, the one who influences the influencer. Let me lead with humility, obedience, and faithfulness. **In Jesus' Name, Amen.**

Chapter 15

Leading When You're Running on Empty

"The whole Israelite community set out from the Desert of Sin, traveling from place to place as the Lord commanded. They camped at Rephidim, but there was no water for the people to drink. So they quarreled with Moses and said, 'Give us water to drink.' Moses replied, 'Why do you quarrel with me? Why do you put the Lord to the test?' … Then Moses cried out to the Lord, 'What am I to do with these people? They are almost ready to stone me.'" - (Exodus 17:1-6 NIV)

Life and Leadership Lesson

Imagine this. You're Moses. You've been leading millions of people through the wilderness. They've already seen miracles. They saw the Red Sea split in two. They saw manna fall from the sky. And still, when they get thirsty, they don't cry out to God. They cry out to you. They're mad, they're desperate, they're loud. They're ready to stone you if you don't come through.

That's crazy pressure.

And Moses is caught in the middle. He's got God above him, people behind him, and no water in sight. He's empty, and the people want him to pour. That's when he cries out, *"What am I supposed to do with these people?"*

Let's be real. Haven't you felt that? Maybe as a father when your kids are looking at you hungry and you don't know how you're gonna feed them. Maybe as a business owner when your employees are expecting checks but your account is dry. Maybe as a leader in ministry when people expect you to have answers, but you're just as confused as they are. Maybe sitting in a cell, everyone depends on you to stay strong, but you feel like you got nothing left to give.

Leadership will drain you if you let it. External pressure is real. Moses isn't the only one who felt this. Elijah got so drained that after calling down fire from heaven, he ran into the desert and begged God to take his life (**1 Kings 19:4**). Paul said in **2 Corinthians 1:8** that he felt *"under great pressure, far beyond our ability to endure, so that we despaired of life itself."*

Even Jesus in Gethsemane felt the crushing weight of expectation, sweating drops of blood (**Luke 22:44**).

But here's the good news. God told Moses to strike the rock, and water poured out for the people (**Exodus 17:6**). That rock was symbolic of Jesus (**1 Corinthians 10:4**). When you're running empty, the answer isn't to dig deeper into yourself, it's to turn to the Rock. He's the source.

The wilderness exposes whether you're leading out of your own strength or God's supply. The truth is, you can't carry it all. You weren't meant to. Moses had to learn that, and so do we, but sometimes we're just some stubborn fools!

So here's the real question for you, are you letting the pressure break you, or are you letting it push you closer to God? Are you leading out of your emptiness, or out of His endless supply? Stay encouraged, fill up on his word, stand on his promises, and keep looking up!

Handle That

This week, don't just try to "push through" when you feel drained. Instead, stop and cry out to God like Moses did. Tell Him exactly how you feel. Then ask Him to provide from His Rock, not your resources. Write down one area where people's expectations are crushing you, and give it to Him.

Take Note

- Where am I feeling the pressure of people's expectations right now?
- Am I trying to provide out of my own strength, or relying on God's provision?
- Who am I leading that needs me to point them to the Rock instead of just myself?

Take It to God

Father, I admit I feel empty sometimes. The pressure of leading, providing, and holding it all together is heavy. Forgive me for trying to lead out of my own strength instead of leaning on You. Teach me to turn to You, my Rock, when I'm dry. Remind me that You're the one who provides, not me. Help me as a leader to stop pretending I have it all, and instead lead by pointing others to You. **In Jesus' Name, Amen.**

Blessed but Burnt Out

"I cannot carry all these people by myself; the burden is too heavy for me. If this is how you are going to treat me, please go ahead and kill me, if I have found favor in your eyes, and do not let me face my own ruin." - (Numbers 11:14-15 NIV)

Life and Leadership Lesson

Let's keep it 100, Moses was blessed, chosen, and handpicked by God, yet he still hit that point where he said, *"I'm done. I can't carry this anymore. Just kill me now."* Boom. That's wild.

And this is Moses we're talking about! The Red Sea splitter. The Ten Commandment receiver. God's friend. If Moses hit that wall, why do we act surprised when we do?

Look, I know you've been there. That place where the weight feels too heavy. Maybe you're running a business and every bill, every paycheck, every decision falls on your shoulders. Maybe you're a father trying to hold your family together, but you're exhausted. Maybe you're locked up and you've been the strong one for everyone else, but deep down you're empty and broken. Maybe you're leading a ministry, but you feel like you got nothing left to give.

That's burnout. And it's real.

Moses wasn't the only one. Elijah called fire from heaven, then ran into the wilderness and begged God to take his life (**1 Kings 19:4**). Jeremiah got so fed up with people mocking him that he said he'd never speak God's word again (**Jeremiah 20:9**). Even Paul admitted he despaired of life itself under the pressure (**2 Corinthians 1:8**). And Jesus Himself, in Gethsemane, fell to the ground under the weight of His mission, sweating blood as He prayed (**Luke 22:44**).

Crazy, right? Even the greatest leaders hit that wall.

But here's the difference, Moses didn't bottle it up. He didn't fake it. He took it to God. That's the leadership lesson right there. When you're burnt out, you can either collapse under it or you can cry out to Jesus with it.

So let me ask you: how do you react when you're burnt out? Do you shut down? Do you lash out at the people you're supposed to lead? Do you run to old habits, addictions, or anger? Or do you take it to the One who can actually handle it?

Here's the truth, burnout isn't a sign you're weak, it's a sign you're human. And it's a reminder that leadership was never meant to be carried alone. Jesus said in **Matthew 11:28-30**, *"Come to me, all you who are weary and burdened, and I will give you rest… For my yoke is easy and my burden is light."*

Boom. That's the game changer. Leaders who last aren't the ones who never burn out, they're the ones who learn to unload their burdens onto Jesus.

Handle That

Don't fake it this week. Write down the areas of your life where you feel burnt out, family, business, ministry, even your personal walk with God. Instead of hiding it, pray about it. Talk to someone you trust about it. And ask yourself, am I leading out of burnout or out of God's rest?

Take Note

- Where in my life do I feel burnt out right now?
- How have I been reacting, by shutting down, lashing out, or leaning on God?
- Who in my life can I trust to share this burden with?
- What's one step I can take today to lay my burnout down at Jesus' feet?

Take It to God

Father, I admit I feel burnt out at times. The weight of leadership, family, and life gets so heavy that I don't know what to do. Forgive me for the times I tried to carry it all myself. Teach me to take my burnout straight to You. Give me rest in my soul, wisdom for my leadership, and strength to keep moving. Thank You that I don't have to carry this burden alone. **In Jesus' Name, Amen.**

Chapter 16

Between the Mountain and the People

"Then Moses went up to God, and the Lord called to him from the mountain..." - (Exodus 19:3 NIV)

"Then the Lord told Moses, 'Go down and prepare the people for my arrival. Consecrate them today and tomorrow, and have them wash their clothing. Be sure they are ready on the third day, for on that day the Lord will come down on Mount Sinai as all the people watch." - (Exodus 19:10-11 NLT)

Life and Leadership Lesson

Moses kept climbing that mountain over and over because God kept calling him up. Imagine the weight of that. You're the middleman between God and a whole nation. Every time God said, **"Moses, come up here,"** Moses went. Then God would say, "Go back down and tell the people this." Back and forth. Mountain to people. People to mountain. Moses was constantly climbing. Up the mountain to meet with God, down the mountain to face the people. Back up for instructions, back down to deal with complaints, sins, doubts, and drama. Repeat. That's tiring, straight up.

Think about it, how many times has God asked you to carry His word, His vision, His correction, His encouragement, back and forth to the people you're leading? Whether you're running a business, leading a ministry, coaching a team, raising a family, or even trying to bring hope to your cell block, leadership often feels like standing between the mountain and the people. That tension is real. You feel pulled in both directions.

Here's the heavy part, Moses had to consecrate himself AND the people. He had to keep going back to God so he wouldn't lose the fire, then return to the people so they could prepare to meet God too. Now, this is what it means to carry the weight of the call. You don't just represent yourself anymore. You represent God to the people, and you represent the people before God.

Now ask yourself, how do you handle that weight? Do you run from it? Do you get tired of climbing the mountain again and again? Or do you keep showing up even when you're drained? Let's be real, some days you feel like saying, "Nah God, I'm good, I'll stay down here this time." But the call won't let you rest. Leadership is climbing when you'd rather quit.

But here's the thing, this is all OLD testament, we're in the NEW testament now. You can go to God directly, you can go up the mountain yourself. You should go up that mountain yourself! You don't need a "Moses" to be that middle man anymore. God speaks to us directly now, you just need to spend that time on that "mountain" whatever it may be for you, and be sensitive to his spirit. You're not the Moses in anyone's life. You need to seek Him directly, you need to answer your call, you need to lead your family, your people, your crew, your employees. You yourself need to spend time on that mountain and return with that glow my boy!

Think about **Abraham**. He had to climb Mount Moriah with Isaac (**Genesis 22**), carrying not only wood but the emotional weight of trusting God with his son. Or **Nehemiah**, who carried the weight of rebuilding walls while the people complained and enemies threatened (**Nehemiah 4**). Or even **Jesus**, who went up Mount of Olives to pray, carrying the weight of our sin before the cross (**Luke 22:39-44**). Leaders always find themselves between the mountain and the people.

But here's the hope, every climb teaches you something. Every trip back and forth builds endurance. Every time you obey and go up, God reveals more of Himself. And every time you come back down, you're carrying something from God that others need. Don't think your climb is wasted. Don't think your leadership tension is meaningless. Nah, God is using it to form you into someone who can be trusted with His presence.

So let me ask you straight up:

- What's the "mountain" God keeps calling you back to? Prayer? His Word? Time in His presence?
- Do you value those moments enough to climb, or are you too busy trying to please the people at the bottom?
- Are you willing to stand in the gap, even when it feels like a burden?

Leadership is costly. But remember, Moses wasn't climbing for nothing. He was climbing to bring God's presence down to the people. That's your role too.

Handle That

Identify your "mountain." Where do you go to hear from God? Is it your prayer closet, your cell, your car, the park, your morning walks? Whatever it is, commit to climbing daily. Don't just lead people, keep meeting with God.

- This week, commit to climbing your "mountain", spend time in prayer, fasting, or Scripture even when it feels heavy.

- Ask yourself: am I carrying what God wants me to bring to my family, my crew, my church, or my business? Or am I only carrying what feels easy?

- Write down how many times Moses climbed up Sinai. Notice how he kept going. Then ask yourself: am I consistent in my calling?

Take Note

- Do you find yourself stuck between God's expectations and people's demands?

- When was the last time you went up the mountain for fresh strength?

- Who am I standing in the gap for right now?

- Do I see my leadership as a burden or a blessing?

- What's one way I can prepare my people, family, business, community, or team, to encounter God?

Take It to God

Father, sometimes the climb feels heavy, and the people feel demanding, but I don't want to quit. Teach me to carry Your presence faithfully. Help me to be a leader who goes up the mountain when You call and comes down with a word that builds, strengthens, and prepares others. Remind me that this tension is part of leadership. Keep me steady so I can bring Your presence to the people You've trusted me with. Teach me to love Your presence on the mountain and to love the people in the valley. You know the weight I carry. Some days it feels too heavy. Forgive me for trying to lead without coming to You first. Teach me to keep climbing the mountain, to seek Your presence, and to carry Your word back to the people You've called me to lead. Give me endurance for the climb and patience for the people. Remind me that I don't have to do it in my strength, but in Yours. **In Jesus' Name, Amen.**

Alone on the Mountain

"The Lord said to Moses, 'Come up to me on the mountain and stay here, and I will give you the tablets of stone, with the law and commands I have written for their instruction.' … Then Moses entered the cloud as he went on up the mountain. And he stayed on the mountain forty days and forty nights." - (Exodus 24:12-18)

Life and Leadership Lesson

This scene is crazy. God calls Moses up the mountain, tells him to come and stay, and Moses ends up there forty days and forty nights. Imagine that…just you, the mountain, and God. No wife, no kids, no crew, no cheering section. Just silence, solitude, and the weight of God's presence.

That's real life for leaders. Everybody wants the platform, but few want the mountain. Because the mountain is lonely. The mountain strips you. The mountain forces you to face yourself and God without distractions.

Now let's get real. Some of y'all reading this know exactly what I'm talking about. The inmate in his cell with nothing but four walls and a Bible, that's your mountain. The pastor who has to smile on Sunday morning but cries alone on Sunday night, that's your mountain. The business owner carrying payroll stress with no one to confide in, that's your mountain. The influencer with thousands of likes but nobody who actually knows their pain and struggle, that's your mountain.

Crazy, right? On top of it all, loneliness don't always look like being physically alone. You can be surrounded by people, and still feel isolated because nobody really gets the weight you carry.

Moses knew that. The people down below were partying, building idols, living reckless. But Moses was up there with God, carrying the responsibility of leading millions. Boom. That's leadership. Sometimes you're up on the mountain while everyone else is chilling in the valley.

And here's the wildest part, God does some of His deepest work on the mountain. It's in the silence that He shapes you. It's in the solitude that He gives vision. It's in the alone moments that He strengthens your spirit. Elijah was alone when God spoke to him in the gentle whisper (**1 Kings 19:11–13**). Jesus Himself would withdraw to lonely places and pray (**Luke 5:16**). Paul was three years in Arabia before stepping fully into his ministry (**Galatians 1:17–18**). Even David, before the crown, was out in the fields writing songs to God in solitude.

So here's the question: how do you handle your mountain? Do you run from the loneliness, fill it with noise, numb it with distractions, or do you press into God and let Him shape you?

Let me talk to the broken leader, the tired parent, the hustler, the dreamer, the one who feels forgotten and overlooked. That lonely season isn't punishment, it's preparation. God ain't wasting your mountain time. He's using it to refine you, to break your pride, to sharpen your faith, and to give you something real to bring down to the people you'll lead.

Moses came down from that mountain glowing (**Exodus 34:29**). That glow didn't come from the crowd, it came from solitude with God. Leaders, your glow, your wisdom, your power, your anointing, it's created out of the mountain seasons nobody else sees.

So what's your mountain right now? Depression? Anxiety? Prison time? Grief? Business struggles? Leadership pressure? Don't waste it. Take it easy... God's got you right where He wants you. Whatever that mountain is, God wants to use you where you're at.

Handle That

Take a day, an hour, or even just 15 minutes this week to step away from the noise. No phone, no TV, no distractions. Just you and God. Journal it. Pray raw. Let Him speak in the silence.

Take Note

- What's the mountain season I'm in right now?
- How have I been reacting, running from the loneliness, or leaning into God?
- What vision or wisdom could God be trying to give me in this season?
- Do I see solitude as weakness or as a chance to glow when I come back down?

Take It to God

Father, thank You for the mountain seasons, even when they feel lonely. Forgive me for trying to run from the silence instead of leaning into it. Teach me to trust that You're shaping me in the solitude. Help me see that what I get on the mountain is what I'll need to lead in the valley. Give me strength, patience, and peace when I feel alone. Remind me that You are always with me, even when no one else is. **In Jesus' Name, Amen.**

Waiting on the Mountain

Life and Leadership Lesson

Moses wasn't just called to climb up. He was called to *wait.* Forty days and forty nights. No shortcuts, no fast tracks, no skipping the process. Just him, the cloud, and the presence of God. That's where the weight of leadership gets real, in the waiting.

See, everybody wants the spotlight, but not everybody wants the silence. The real leaders get shaped in the cloud, not the crowd. Moses disappears for over a month, and the people at the bottom of the mountain think he's dead. They lose patience and build a golden calf. But Moses is in God's presence getting the blueprint for a whole nation. Sometimes your "waiting on the mountain" season will make people question you, doubt you, or even turn on you. But you can't trade their pressure for His presence.

For the homie in prison, you know what waiting feels like. Counting days. Feeling forgotten. Wondering if anybody remembers you. But what if your "forty" is God's training ground? What if your cell is your Sinai? God ain't wasting it. He's writing on the tablet of your heart right now.

For the entrepreneur, the CEO, the parent, the pastor, waiting feels like a waste. You're wired to move, to grind, to fix. But the question is, are you willing to let God do more in your silence than you could do in your hustle? Boom. That's leadership.

And don't forget this, every "forty" in the Bible was about preparation. Forty days of rain in Noah's flood (**Genesis 7:17**). Forty years in the desert to humble Israel (**Deuteronomy 8:2**). Jesus fasted forty days before stepping into His ministry (**Matthew 4:1-2**). Moses wasn't the only one. Leaders throughout Scripture had to endure their "forty." And so will you.

So let me ask you:

- Do you run from the waiting, or do you embrace it?
- Are you letting God shape you, or are you building golden calves because you're restless?
- Do you trust His timing, or do you think you gotta make it happen yourself?

Waiting on the mountain is never wasted. It's where God fills you so you can lead others when it's time to come down.

Handle That

- Identify your mountain. Where can you step away and give God time to speak?
- Write down the areas where you've been impatient, and ask God to flip that into faith.
- Commit to giving God the silence He needs to download His blueprint into your life.

Take Note

- When was the last time I let God keep me in a "forty" season without rushing out?
- What idols have I built out of impatience while waiting?
- Do I believe God's presence is enough, even when nothing seems to be happening?

Take It to God

Father, I don't always like waiting, but I know that waiting on the mountain is where You shape leaders. Forgive me for rushing ahead or building idols when I get impatient. Teach me to trust the silence and the process. Fill me with Your presence so that when I come down, I come down carrying Your vision, not just my ideas. Help me embrace the waiting, because I know it's not wasted. **In Jesus' Name, Amen.**

Chapter 17

When the Idols Fall

"And he took the calf the people had made and burned it in the fire; then he ground it to powder, scattered it on the water and made the Israelites drink it." - (Exodus 32:20)

Life and Leadership Lesson

Let's keep it 100. The people got restless, they didn't see Moses coming back, and they pressured Aaron into building a golden calf. Boom! That's wild. After seeing the Red Sea split, manna falling from the sky, water from rocks, they still built an idol. That's human nature, right? When we feel like God's taking too long, we start building our own thing to worship.

Now before you clown them, ask yourself, what's your golden calf? Don't play. Is it money? Success? Followers? The street rep? That relationship? Your career? Maybe it's even ministry itself. Anything that steals God's spot in your life is a calf. And calves don't always look ugly. Sometimes they look shiny, popular, and respectable. But if it's taking God's place, it's gotta go bro.

Moses came down, saw the calf, and he didn't say, "Let's just push it to the side." Nah. He destroyed it, burned it, smashed it to dust, and made the people taste the bitterness of their sin. Boom. Real leaders don't ignore idols, they deal with them head on.

Let me make it personal. If you walked back into your home, your job, your church, or even your cellblock and saw a golden calf built, how would you react? Would you ignore it? Would you join in? Or would you call it out?

Parents, are you willing to confront idols in your kids' lives? Pastors, will you call out the idols in your church? Business leaders, are you bold enough to check the culture when money becomes god? Street leaders, do you have the guts to tell your people that what they're chasing is killing them?

This is heavy because idols ain't just "out there," they're in here. In our own hearts. **Ezekiel 14:3** says people set up idols in their own hearts. Jesus said in ***Matthew 6:24, "You cannot serve two masters."*** So the question is, who's really on the throne?

Idols always demand a cost, but they never deliver what they promise. They give you hype for a minute, then leave you empty the next minute. And if you're a leader, you can't afford to worship idols, because what you bow to, your people will bow to.

So what's your golden calf? Are you brave enough to smash it, even if everyone else wants to protect it? That's the call of leadership.

Handle That

Call out one idol in your life this week. Be honest with yourself. Then pray and literally name it out loud before God: "This is my calf." Ask Him to burn it down so you can lead free.

Take Note

- What golden calf have I built in my own life when I got impatient with God?
- Am I willing to confront idols in the people I lead, even if it makes me unpopular?
- Do my family, my business, or my church see me smashing idols or hiding them?
- What's the steps I need to take this week to tear down an idol in my life?

Take It to God

Father, please remove anything in my life that takes Your place. Show me the idols I've built, even the ones I've ignored or justified. Give me the courage to smash them down and lead others to do the same. Teach me to put You first in every area of my life, and to be a leader who destroys idols instead of building them. **In Jesus' Name, Amen.**

While You Were Gone

"When the people saw that Moses was so long in coming down from the mountain, they gathered around Aaron and said, 'Come, make us gods who will go before us…' Then the Lord said to Moses, 'Go down, because your people, whom you brought up out of Egypt, have become corrupt. They have been quick to turn away…" - Exodus 32:1, 7-10

Life and Leadership Lesson

Let's keep it real, when the leader's gone, stuff gets messy. Moses was up on the mountain, face-to-face with God, getting instructions for the people. But while he was gone, they got impatient. They started talking, "Yo Aaron, we don't know what happened to Moses. Make us some gods we can follow." Boom. That's crazy. In just a little time, they forgot all the miracles, all the deliverance, all the power they had seen.

And that's real life. How many times do people get impatient when leadership steps away? When the boss isn't in the office. When the pastor takes a break. When accountability is gone. People start slipping, drifting, falling into old habits. They build their own "golden calves", idols of money, status, sex, drugs, comfort, whatever looks shiny enough to distract them.

Let me ask you, what idols have you built in the silence? When leadership wasn't watching? When God felt far?

But here's the wild part. God saw it all. While Moses was still up on the mountain, God said, "Go down, your people are wilding out." The people thought no one was watching, but God was. Boom. That's a leadership lesson right there, even when you're not present, God is.

Then it gets heavier. God tells Moses He's ready to wipe the people out and start over with just him. Imagine that. Most leaders would've said, "Bet, I'll take that deal. Less stress. Fewer complainers." But Moses? Nah. He stood in the gap. He told God, "If You destroy them, the Egyptians will clown and say You brought them out just to kill them. Keep Your promise. Have mercy." That's leadership. That's intercession. That's putting others before yourself, even when they don't deserve it.

Crazy, right? Moses didn't just fight for the people when they loved him. He fought for them when they betrayed God and went against him. Leaders don't just lead when it's easy, they stand in the gap when it's hard.

And that's the same for us. As a leader, father, business owner, or even as an inmate leading in the yard, you're gonna face moments where people let you down. They'll backstab you, doubt you, or turn to their own idols. Question is: are you gonna quit on them, or are you gonna fall on your face like Moses and pray for them anyway?

Jesus did it best. On the cross, He prayed for the same people mocking Him, **"Father, forgive them, for they know not what they do" (Luke 23:34).** Paul did it when the churches he planted turned messy, he kept praying for them **(Philippians 1:3-6).** True leadership is about interceding for people even when they don't deserve it.

Peep this, while you were gone, people may have failed. But as a leader, your job is to step back in, not with condemnation, but with intercession. Don't quit on the ones God trusted you to lead.

Handle That

Think about someone who disappointed you while you were "gone." Maybe you left for a season, maybe you gave them responsibility, maybe you just weren't there to guide them. Instead of cutting them off, pray for them this week. Intercede like Moses did.

Take Note

- Who in my life has failed when I wasn't around?
- How do I usually respond when people disappoint me, with anger or with prayer?
- What golden calves have I built in my own life when God felt absent?
- Am I willing to intercede for others even when they don't deserve it?

Take It to God

Father, thank You for showing me that leadership is about more than presence, it's about intercession. Forgive me for the idols I've built when I got impatient, and forgive me for giving up on people when they failed. Teach me to stand in the gap, to pray for others even when they don't deserve it. Give me the heart of Moses, the boldness of Paul, and the love of Jesus to lead with mercy. **In Jesus' Name, Amen.**

Chapter 18

The Cost of Compromise

"Then Pharaoh summoned Moses and Aaron and said, 'Go, sacrifice to your God here in the land.'" - (Exodus 8:25)

Life and Leadership Lesson

Check this out. Pharaoh hit Moses with a slick offer: "Go ahead and worship your God… but do it here, in the land." Sounds harmless, right? But that's compromise. Pharaoh was basically saying, "You can do your thing, just don't leave my system. Don't fully obey. Stay half in, half out."

Boom. That's wild. Because that's the same trick the enemy uses on us. He don't come at you all the way like, "Stop serving God." Nah, he whispers, "Just tone it down. Don't go all in. You can worship, but keep it simple. Take it easy, don't take it too serious. Don't leave Egypt all the way."

And that's the cost of compromise, it always keeps you chained up even when you think you're free.

Let me ask you, what are the little compromises in your life? That "harmless" relationship you know ain't right? That shady business move that makes you more money but robs your integrity? That one thing you say you'll quit "one day" but that day never comes.

Who else compromised?

- Samson compromised with Delilah and it cost him his strength and his sight (**Judges 16**).
- Solomon compromised by marrying women who worshiped other gods. It didn't happen overnight, but over time his heart drifted, and the kingdom split (**1 Kings 11**).
- Lot compromised by pitching his tent near Sodom. He thought he could live close without being corrupted, but eventually he was sitting at the city gates like one of them (**Genesis 13:12, 19:1**).

Crazy, right? Every one of them thought the little compromise wasn't a big deal. But compromise is like a weed, leave it alone, and it grows until it chokes everything out.

Leaders, this is where it gets real. As a father, are you letting little compromises slide at home? As a Pastor, are you watering down truth so people stay comfortable? As a business owner, are you cutting corners because you think you can get away with it and others do it so easily? As someone sitting in a cell, are you still messing with the same mindset that got you locked up?

Compromise is dangerous because it doesn't just affect you, it affects everyone connected to you. Moses refused Pharaoh's deal because he knew half-obedience is still disobedience. Real leadership is being bold enough to say, "Nah, I'm not settling. I'm going all the way."

So what's the Pharaoh in your life have to offer you? Where's he telling you, "Stay here, don't go too far"? At some point you gotta decide if you're gonna keep up the compromise or start fresh.

Handle That

Find that one thing where you've been compromising. Write it down. Then ask yourself, "What will this cost me if I keep it up?" Then make the decision today to cut it off before it grows.

Take Note

- What small compromises have I been justifying?
- How have those compromises already affected my leadership?
- Am I choosing comfort over obedience?
- What bold step of obedience do I need to take this week?

Take It to God

Father, forgive me for the times I've settled for compromise. Show me the areas where I've been half-obedient, half-committed, and teach me to go all in with You. Give me the courage to say no to Pharaoh's offers, no to the enemy's traps, and yes to full obedience. Make me a leader who refuses to settle, no matter the cost. **In Jesus' Name, Amen.**

Disobedience and Consequences, When You Know Better, But Still Do It Anyway

"But the Lord said to Moses and Aaron, "Because you did not trust in Me enough to honor Me as holy in the sight of the Israelites, you will not bring this community into the land I give them." - Numbers 20:12

Life and Leadership Lesson

Disobedience is one of those things that hits harder the older you get, because the more you know, the more you're accountable for. Moses found that out the hard way.

God told him to *speak* to the rock, but he *struck* it instead, twice. Water still came out, but that one act of frustration, that one emotional decision, cost him the Promised Land. Crazy, right? After forty years of miracles, mountains, and manna, Moses didn't cross over. Not because he didn't believe God could, but because for that moment, he stopped trusting how God said to do it. That's leadership at its most real, even one moment of disobedience can change the course of your destiny.

And this wasn't the first time the people of God dropped the ball either. Remember when Moses went up the mountain and the people couldn't wait? They built a golden calf and started wilding out, dancing, worshiping a statue made from their own jewelry. When Moses came down, he smashed those stone tablets, burned the idol, ground it into powder, mixed it with water, and made them drink it **(Exodus 32:19-20)**. Thousands died that day. Boom. Consequences.

The Hebrews disobeyed over and over, complaining about manna, whining about going back to Egypt, testing God in the wilderness. Every time they doubted, something was delayed. What could've been an 11-day journey took 40 years because of disobedience **(Deuteronomy 1:2-3)**. Forty years of walking in circles, all because they couldn't stop second-guessing God.

Let's be real, disobedience ain't just about doing what's wrong. It's also about *not doing* what's right. **James 4:17** says, ***"If anyone knows the good they ought to do and doesn't do it, it is sin."*** That one hurts, it cuts deep because it exposes the other side of disobedience: when we stay silent instead of speaking, when we ignore God's nudge, when we keep saying, "One day, I'll do it."

We'll be judged not just for what we *did*, but for what we *didn't do*. Jesus said in ***Luke 12:47***: ***"The servant who knows his master's will and doesn't get ready or do what his master wants will be beaten with many blows."*** In other words, knowing better and not doing better ain't ignorance, it's rebellion.

It's not just about Moses either. Check out the Word, every time people tried to do things their own way, the fallout was real:

- Adam and Eve disobeyed one command, and paradise turned into pain (***Genesis 3***).
- Saul played politics with obedience, lost his kingdom (***1 Samuel 15***).
- Jonah ran from his assignment, ended up in the belly of a fish (***Jonah 1***).
- Lot's wife looked back when God said "don't," and turned into a pillar of salt (***Genesis 19:26***).
- Ananias and Sapphira lied to God and dropped in the same service (***Acts 5***).

Disobedience might feel small in the moment, but the consequences echo. And it ain't because God's petty, it's because obedience is the proof of love **(John 14:15)**.

And the fallout? It's real. Disobedience brings consequences that hit every area of life:

- Jail, because you knew the law and still broke it. (You know who you are.)
- Getting fired, because you ignored instruction or refused correction.
- Divorce, because pride made you stop listening and loving.
- Broken relationships, because you couldn't admit when you were wrong.
- Sickness and stress, because you ignored what God said about rest and self-control. Yup.

Disobedience don't just cost your position, it costs your peace.

Even Jesus made it clear that obedience isn't optional. In ***John 14:15***, He said, ***"If you love Me, keep My commandments."*** That's heavy bro. He didn't say, "If you love Me, agree with My commandments." He said ***keep them***. Love is proven through obedience. And He backed it up Himself. **Philippians 2:8** says, ***"He humbled Himself and became obedient to death, even death on a cross."*** Jesus showed us that obedience sometimes hurts, but it always honors God.

So yeah, disobedience is a big deal. It's what kicked Adam and Eve out of paradise, what drowned Pharaoh's army, what delayed Israel's promise, what took Saul's crown, and what kept Moses out of Canaan. It's what breaks homes, ruins callings, ends relationships, and leaves blessings unfinished.

And here's the part we don't talk about enough, you can look like you're walking in purpose while still being disobedient. Moses hit that rock, water still flowed. People drank. It looked successful. But God wasn't pleased. You can get results and still be wrong. The goal isn't results, it's *obedience*. That's a reminder that just because something works, it doesn't mean that God is in it.

So I gotta ask, where are you still striking when God said speak? Where are you dragging your feet when He said move? What has He told you to do that you keep putting off? And what's it already costing you?

Disobedience always costs something. Sometimes it's your reputation. Sometimes it's your opportunity. And sometimes, like Moses, it's your next level.

Handle That

- Be honest with yourself. Where in your life are you ignoring what God clearly told you to do
- Write down one act of obedience you've been putting off, and do it this week.
- Make peace with whoever you've hurt by disobedience, pride can't heal what humility won't face.
- Ask God to show you the areas where partial obedience has become your normal, and fix it before it costs more.

Take Note

- What clear instructions from God have you delayed or ignored because of fear or pride?
- Have you confused "results" with "obedience"?
- How would your life change if you started obeying God immediately instead of negotiating with Him?
- What's one area where your disobedience has already caused damage, and what can you do to make it right?

Take It to God

Father, forgive me for every time I've disobeyed You, for the things I did that I knew were wrong, and for the things I didn't do when You clearly told me to. I don't want to forfeit my promise like Moses did. Teach me to value obedience over emotion, over convenience, and over comfort. Remind me that real love means obedience, not just belief. Heal what my disobedience has broken, in my home, my relationships, my body, and my purpose. Give me the strength to follow Your voice fully, no matter how hard it gets. **In Jesus' Name, Amen.**

Chapter 19

Stop Trying to Please Everybody

"When Moses approached the camp and saw the calf and the dancing, his anger burned and he threw the tablets out of his hands... He said to Aaron, 'What did these people do to you, that you led them into such great sin?' Aaron answered, 'Do not be angry, my lord. You know how prone these people are to evil." - (Exodus 32:19-24)

"Am I now trying to win the approval of human beings, or of God?... If I were still trying to please people, I would not be a servant of Christ." - (Galatians 1:10)

Life and Leadership Lesson

Here's the deal, you will never be able to make everybody happy. Not in business, not in ministry, not on the block, not even in your own family, so take it easy! If you try, you'll end up like Aaron at the foot of the mountain, building golden calves just to keep people off your back.

Let's be real. Some of us are addicted to approval. We want likes, claps, compliments, pats on the back. We want our name shouted out in the meeting, the sermon, or the streets. But here's the problem, people will switch up on you real quick. Remember how they did Jesus? The same crowd that yells "Hosanna" will yell "Crucify Him" a week later.

Aaron gave in to pressure and was the ultimate people pleaser. Instead of standing his ground, he got pressured into compromise. He made them a golden calf because he didn't want to disappoint. He straight up lost sight of God's call and started living for the crowd's approval.

I know this struggle. I've been there. Wanting everyone to like me, to support me, to ride with me. But the truth is, if you're leading right, some people are gonna be mad. Some will walk away. Some will misunderstand you. Some will straight up hate. That's part of leadership.

So let me ask you this, are you surrounding yourself with yes-men? People who only tell you what you want to hear? Are you making decisions to keep the peace instead of walking in truth? Are you more worried about losing social media followers than losing God's favor and presence?

Leaders, listen. God didn't call you to be popular. He called you to be faithful. And sometimes faithfulness looks like standing alone. Sometimes it looks like saying no when everybody wants you to say yes. Sometimes it looks like disappointing people so you don't disappoint God.

If Paul said he couldn't be a servant of Christ and still chase human approval, then neither can we. You can't live for the claps of the crowd and the call of God at the same time.

So here's the challenge: Stop bending. Stop watering down. Stop living for the validation of those that don't even care about you. You don't need to prove yourself to anybody but God.

Handle That

Do a gut check this week. Where in your life are you compromising just to keep people happy? Write it down. Then make a decision, God's approval over people's applause.

Take Note

- Where are you trying to win people's approval instead of God's?
- Who in your circle only tells you what you want to hear instead of what you need to hear?
- What would change if you cared more about being faithful than being popular?

Take It to God

Father, I admit that I've chased people's approval before yours. I've wanted people to like me more than I've wanted to obey You. Forgive me for the times I've compromised just to please the crowd. Teach me to stand firm, even when it costs me popularity. Surround me with people who tell me the truth, not just what I want to hear. Help me live for Your applause, not theirs. **In Jesus' Name, Amen.**

Chapter 20

There Will Be Naysayers

"Moses answered, 'What if they do not believe me or listen to me and say, 'The Lord did not appear to you'?" - (Exodus 4:1)

"They came as a group to oppose Moses and Aaron and said to them, 'You have gone too far! The whole community is holy, every one of them, and the Lord is with them. Why then do you set yourselves above the Lord's assembly?" - (Numbers 16:3)

"Has the Lord spoken only through Moses? they asked. Hasn't he also spoken through us? And the Lord heard this." - (Numbers 12:2)

Life and Leadership Lesson

Leadership ain't for the thin-skinned. You're gonna have doubters and haters. You're gonna have backbiters. Even Jesus had Judas sitting at His table. Moses had the same thing.

It started early. Before Moses even got to Pharaoh, he was already asking God, *"What if they don't believe me? What if they think I'm making this whole thing up?"* Moses was already afraid of the naysayers popping off. And God's answer was simple: "I'll be with you. I'll give you the signs." Meaning, you don't need their validation when you've got My presence and permission.

Haters gonna hate and later on, Moses' *own cousin*, Korah, stepped up with 250 men to challenge his leadership. Imagine that. Your own bloodline building an army to take you down. Korah basically said, "Moses, you're not special. Who made you the leader? We're just as holy as you." That's straight rebellion. And Moses didn't hit back with pride or ego. He fell on his face before God and let God handle it.

And if that wasn't enough, his own brother and sister, Aaron and Miriam - even they started talking behind his back. Family drama. They didn't like who he married, they didn't like how he led, and they straight up questioned his authority. God Himself had to check them. He called them out and said, *"Why were you not afraid to speak against My servant Moses?"*

No matter how anointed, called, or chosen you are, there will be naysayers. People will question you. Family will doubt you. Friends will turn on you. Whole groups will rally against you. Expect it. Don't be surprised when it comes.

But here's the key, don't fight naysayers with your flesh. Fight them by falling on your face. Moses didn't build an army back. He didn't start swinging. He fell down before God, and God fought for him.

No matter what industry you're in, someone will have something to say about you. There will always be that one co-worker, that one guy on the yard who feels threatened by you, that one dude who may not understand the favor on your life that spreads lies about you. Stay focused, keep your eyes on Jesus.

So, who are the naysayers in your life? Who's been questioning your call, doubting your vision, whispering about you behind your back? And how have you been reacting? Do you clap back on social media? Do you get bitter? Or do you fall on your face and take it to God?

A true leader expects naysayers, but doesn't let them knock him off course.

Handle That

Think about the naysayers in your life right now. Write their names down, but instead of plotting revenge or clapping back, pray over those names. Ask God to fight for you and teach you to lead above the noise.

Take Note

- Who in your life has doubted or spoken against your calling?
- How have you been reacting, in the flesh or in the Spirit?
- What would change if, like Moses, you fell on your face before God instead of fighting back?

Take It to God

Father, I know there will be naysayers. People who doubt me, question me, or even turn against me. It hurts even deeper when it's the people I trusted most. But I don't want to fight in my flesh. Teach me to respond like Moses, to fall on my face and take it to You. Remind me that my calling comes from You, not from them. Protect my heart from bitterness and help me stay focused on the assignment. Fight for me when I'm surrounded by doubters, and let my life be proof that You called me. **In Jesus' Name, Amen.**

Chapter 21

Face to Face

"The Lord would speak to Moses face to face, as one speaks to a friend. Then Moses would return to the camp, but his young aide Joshua son of Nun did not leave the tent." - (Exodus 33:11)

Life and Leadership Lesson

This one right here hits hard. Out of all the ways Moses could've been described, leader of millions, miracle worker, deliverer of Israel, the one title that stands out most is *friend of God.* Think about that. The Creator of the universe spoke to him face to face, like a friend. That's intimacy. That's relationship. That's what gave Moses the strength to lead.

But here's what's even crazier, Joshua, the assistant, the understudy, the number two, he loved God's presence so much that when Moses left the tent, Joshua stayed. He wasn't even the guy in charge yet. He had no spotlight, no fame, no title. But he was hungry. He lingered where God was. No wonder he was ready when it was his time to lead.

That's a lesson for all of us. Just because you're chosen, doesn't mean you can coast. Just because you're anointed, doesn't mean you can skip time with God. Being a leader doesn't make you exempt from the basics. If anything, it makes intimacy with Him even more important.

Leaders, inmates, CEOs, hustlers, pastors, influencers - I need to ask you, are you making space to sit face to face with God? Or are you so busy running meetings, building businesses, preaching sermons, chasing likes, or hustling for respect that you skip the presence?

For real though, some of us treat God like a hotline, only calling when we're in trouble. Some of us dip in for a quick prayer just to check the box, then rush out. But Joshua teaches us something different, stay. Linger in it bro. Don't be in such a hurry to leave God's presence.

Keep it real, people can tell when you've been with God. Moses' face literally glowed. You can't fake that glow. No amount of filters on Instagram, no new business card, no fancy title can replace the shine of someone who's been face to face with God.

So let me ask you, do people around you see that glow? Does your family, your employees, your cellmate, your congregation, your friends, do they see the evidence that you've been with Him? Or do you look just as drained, bitter, and restless as everybody else?

Joshua wasn't leading yet, but he was preparing. Maybe that's you right now. Maybe you're not the boss, not the pastor, not the one in the spotlight. But if you'll learn to love God's presence now, when it's your time, you'll be ready.

Handle That

Don't rush God. Set a time this week to just sit in His presence. No agenda, no rush, no checklist. Be like Joshua, stay even after everyone else leaves.

Take Note

- Are you treating God like an emergency contact instead of a best friend?
- Do you crave His presence more than success, recognition, or comfort?
- How can you build a habit of lingering, like Joshua, instead of rushing out?

Take It to God

Father, forgive me for all the times I've rushed past You to chase other things. Teach me to love Your presence like Moses did, and to linger like Joshua did. I don't just want to be known as a leader, I want to be known as Your friend. Give me a hunger to stay with You longer, even when nobody else sees. Let my life shine with the glow of Your presence. **In Jesus' Name, Amen.**

Show Me Your Glory

"Then Moses said, 'Now show me Your glory." - Exodus 33:18

Life and Leadership Lesson

That one line right there? That's everything. Moses didn't ask God for a bigger army. He didn't ask for more miracles. He said, "God, I just wanna see You."

That hits me deep. How many times do we pray for things from God instead of just wanting more of God? We ask Him to open doors, bless our hustle, fix what's broken, but when's the last time you said, "Lord, I just wanna know You better"?

Moses had already seen wild stuff, the sea split, manna falling from the sky, fire at night, a cloud by day, but he wanted something deeper. He wanted the presence. The real thing. The kind of encounter that changes who you are, not just what you do. We should all want that!

And that's leadership right there. Because leadership without presence is just performance.

You can build platforms and followings, throw events, speak to crowds, but if God ain't in it, it's empty. Moses said, **"If Your presence doesn't go with us, don't send us from here." (Exodus 33:15)** That dude understood the assignment.

Now look, Moses wasn't the only one who asked for God's glory.

In **Isaiah 6**, **Isaiah** saw the Lord sitting on His throne, high and lifted up, and his response wasn't, "That's dope!", it was, **"Woe is me, I'm unclean."** That's what real presence does. It exposes and transforms you.

Elijah met God on Mount Horeb **(1 Kings 19)**. There was wind, an earthquake, and fire, but God wasn't in any of that. Then came a whisper. You feel that? The glory ain't always loud. Sometimes it's quiet. Sometimes it's that still small voice telling you, "I'm still with you."

Peter, James, and **John** saw Jesus' face shine like the sun on the Mount of Transfiguration **(Matthew 17)**. **Paul** got knocked off his horse and blinded by the light of Christ **(Acts 9)**. **John** saw heaven open and described it like nothing he'd ever seen before **(Revelation 1)**.

All those moments? Different people, different times, same truth, when you really encounter God's glory, you don't stay the same. You start walking different. You start leading different. You stop chasing crowds and start chasing calling.

See, the glory of God ain't about the spotlight, it's about surrender. It's when you stop asking, "God, bless *what* I'm doing," and start saying, "God, let me be *where* You're blessing." That's when leaders shift from being driven by success to being moved by Spirit.

When you lead, it's easy to get caught up chasing results, the numbers, the wins, the growth. But Moses teaches us something deeper: before you lead people, you gotta learn how to sit with God. Every real leader has that "mountain moment", the space where it's just you and Him. That's where clarity comes from. That's where vision is born.

If you lose that connection, you start moving on impulse instead of instruction. You start reacting instead of responding. The glory of God reminds you who's really in charge. It humbles you, fills you, and guides you. When God shows up, He doesn't just change your situation, He changes you.

Handle That

Stop rushing ahead of God. Slow down and sit with Him. I personally have struggled with this.

Before you make that move, before you say *yes* to that next thing, ask, "God, are You in this?"

Don't chase the spotlight, chase the secret place. That's where real leaders are made.

Take Note

- When's the last time you really felt God's presence?
- What's distracting you from sitting still long enough to hear His whisper?
- Are you leading from presence or pressure?
- If God asked you to stay still for a season, could you do it?

Take It to God

Father, I don't just want to talk about You, I wanna walk with You. I don't want the stage if You're not in the room. Show me Your glory, the kind that humbles me and heals me. Make me a leader who waits for Your voice and moves when You move. Teach me to value Your presence more than my plans. If You're not in it, I don't want it. **In Jesus' Name, Amen.**

Chapter 22

If God Ain't in It, I Don't Want It

"Then Moses said to him, 'If your Presence does not go with us, do not send us up from here. How will anyone know that you are pleased with me and with your people unless you go with us? What else will distinguish me and your people from all the other people on the face of the earth?'" - (Exodus 33:15-16)

Life and Leadership Lesson

Moses had a wild conversation with God right here. God told him, "I'll send an angel to go with you, but I'm not going with you." And Moses said, "Nah. That ain't it. If You don't go with us, I don't want to go." Boom. That's real leadership.

Think about that. God was offering success without His presence. Promises without His partnership. And Moses said, "If You're not there, it's pointless."

Crazy, right? How many times do we chase opportunities or even ministry success without checking if God's in it? How many of us say yes to money, clout, relationships, business deals, or even church positions without asking if God's presence is riding shotgun? I know I've made moves without first praying for God to be in it and it has never turned out successful.

Here's the truth, God's presence is what makes the difference. That's what set Moses apart. Not his skill, not his résumé, not his leadership training. **Exodus 33:11** says he spoke to God face-to-face, like a friend. That's why he could lead. That's why the people followed.

So let me make it personal: have you asked God to go with you? Into that new business? Into that new relationship? Into that courtroom? Into that project? Into that ministry? Or are you just hoping His angel covers it while you run ahead?

David knew this too. In **Psalm 51:11**, after he messed up, he cried out, ***"Don't take Your Holy Spirit from me."*** He wasn't worried about losing his crown or his army. He was scared of losing God's presence. That's the heart of a leader. It's a scary thing when God has removed his hand from your life.

Joshua got it too. In **Exodus 33:11**, after Moses left the tent of meeting, Joshua stayed behind. He wanted more of God's presence, even as the "number two guy." That hunger is what made him the next leader.

So I'll ask you, are you chasing the angel or the presence? Are you chasing the promise or the Promiser? What are you really after?

Because let's be real: without God's presence, all the success in the world is just noise. But with His presence, even if you're locked up, broke, or overlooked, you're rich.

Handle That

This week, before you make a move, pause and ask God: "Are You in this?" If He's not, don't go. If He is, then go all in and be all about it. Write down a few areas of your life right now, work, family, ministry, hustle, and pray specifically, "God, I want Your presence in this, not just results."

Take Note

- Where in my life have I been chasing success without God's presence?
- Have I been satisfied with the "angel" instead of asking for God Himself?
- Do people know I've been with God, or do they just see my grind and my hustle?

Take It to God

Father, I don't want to move without You. Forgive me for the times I've chased blessings, opportunities, and success without first seeking Your presence. Teach me to value You above everything else. Let people know I've been with You, not because of my title or achievements, but because Your presence shines through me. Go with me into my family, my work, my ministry, and my struggles. Without You, it's not worth it. **In Jesus' Name, Amen.**

Chapter 23

That Glow

"When Moses came down from Mount Sinai, with the two tablets of the testimony in his hand as he came down from the mountain, Moses did not know that the skin of his face shone because he had been talking with God." - (Exodus 34:29 ESV)

Life and Leadership Lesson

Moses came down from meeting with God and he didn't even know he was glowing. He wasn't trying to look holy. He wasn't forcing a vibe. Moses didn't realize his face was shining. He wasn't in front of a mirror, he wasn't trying to impress anybody, he wasn't chasing likes, he was just fresh out of God's presence. And the glow that glow just hit. Everybody else could see it. He simply spent time with God and the effect showed up on his face. People noticed. Leaders, listen. Presence changes your presence. Time with God leaves a mark you just can't fake.

That's the thing about time with God. You might not notice it right away, but people around you will. The way you talk and the way you move changes. The way you respond to problems changes. You carry something different, something real that you can't fake. And let's be real, the world is full of fake. Fake smiles, fake confidence, fake leadership, fake loyalty. But you can't fake the glow.

Your glow sets the tone. If you carry anxiety, your team will carry it too. If you carry hope, they will breathe easier. If you carry holiness, compromise loses air. Moses glowed after the tent of meeting **(Exodus 33:11)** and the mountain. Private devotion turned into public influence. That is leadership.

Let's keep it real. Do people notice anything different after you have been with God, or do they just see stress, grind, and attitude. When you walk into the shop, the classroom, the yard, the meeting, the kitchen, does peace walk in with you. Or do people brace for impact because you bring chaos.

Ask yourself: what's coming off of me when I walk into the room? Do I bring peace or stress? Do people feel encouraged or drained? Do my kids feel loved when I come home, or do they feel the weight of my frustration? Do my employees feel secure with me leading, or do they feel like they're one mistake away from me blowing up? Do my people see someone who's been with God, or someone who's been with their ego? Remember, the longer a tea bag sits in the cup, the stronger the tea. The longer you sit in the word and his presence, the stronger your faith will be. That glow is about the fruit of that secret place.

Scripture backs this heavy.

- **Acts 4:13** says the leaders saw Peter and John were ordinary men, but they recognized they had been with Jesus. Ordinary plus Jesus still turns heads.
- **Psalm 34:5** says, "Those who look to Him are radiant." That is glow talk.
- **2 Corinthians 3:7-18** explains Moses' glow and then says we, with unveiled faces, behold the Lord and are transformed from glory to glory. No veil. Real change.
- **Matthew 17** shows Jesus transfigured. Glory revealed.

- **Matthew 5:14-16** says you are the light of the world. Not someday. Now. Let it shine.
- **Philippians 2:15** says shine like stars in a crooked world. That is Monday morning leadership.
- **2 Corinthians 2:15** says we are the aroma of Christ. People should catch a scent of Jesus when you step in the room.

Now let's get personal. Have you lost the glow? Be honest. Leaders get weak. Inmates battle boredom and bitterness. Business owners drown in deadlines. Parents get thin. Pastors get numb. It happens. Samson woke up and did not realize the Spirit had departed (**Judges 16:20**). The church in Ephesus had hustle but lost their first love (**Revelation 2:4**). Martha was serving hard while Mary chose the better part, at Jesus' feet (**Luke 10:38-42**). Busy is not the same as bright.

What dims the glow.

- **Unconfessed sin**. It fogs the soul. (Take the trash out)
- **Performing for people**. You start posing instead of praying. (Don't be a "poser".)
- **Isolation without God**. Alone, but not abiding (**John 15:4-5**). (Not the kind of "alone" time you want)

How do you get the glow back? Not by trying harder to look spiritual. You get it back where Moses got it. In God's presence. In repentance that is real (**1 John 1:9**). In worship that is honest. In the Word that reads you back (**Hebrews 4:12**). In obedience that costs something (**John 14:21**). In community that sharpens you (**Proverbs 27:17**). The glow is earned by being in his presence, it's not a mask you paint on.

- **For my brother in the cell**. Your bunk can be an altar. Open the Word. Pray in whispers if you have to. Let God light you up in the darkest tier. Men will notice the peace on you.

- **For the entrepreneur**. Before you open the laptop, open your Bible. Bring clarity into the boardroom that you found in the prayer room.

- **For the creative**. Let your time with God shape your art, not the algorithm.

- **For the pastor**. Do not trade secret place for stage time. Sheep can tell when a shepherd has not been with *the* Shepherd.

Ask yourself.

- Have I replaced being with God with "working for God"? (hits me hard)
- When people describe me, do they mention joy, peace, gentleness. That sounds like **Galatians 5:22-23**. Or do they only mention your grind?
- If I lost the glow, where did I lose it? Sin? Shame?
- What one habit would most quickly restore my glow in this season?

Here's the thing. Guard your secret place. Schedule solitude like it is a meeting with your top client. Fast from noise. Keep short accounts with God. Pray the Psalms when your words run out. Read the Gospels until Jesus' tone starts to shape yours. Serve someone in secret **(Matthew 6:4)**. The glow returns when the heart returns.

And remember, the glow is not for flex. It is for service. Moses came down shining, then he went right back to shepherding a messy people. Your glow is for the good of others. It points people to the One you have been with, not to you.

This ain't just about Moses. Look at Stephen in **Acts 6:15** - when he was on trial, staring death in the face, the Bible says his face looked like an angel. **That glow wasn't fear, it wasn't panic, it was peace. Why? Because he was full of the Holy Spirit.** Look at Peter and John in Acts **4:13**. The leaders could tell they weren't educated or trained, but they recognized one thing: *these men had been with Jesus.*

Crazy, right? They didn't have diplomas or resumes. They had presence. God's presence. And that outshines credentials every time.

Now let me keep it real. Too many leaders today are chasing platforms instead of presence. We'd rather post about being busy for God than sit quietly with God. We'd rather chase business deals, church growth, likes and shares, than chase the glow that comes from intimacy with Him. But Moses shows us something, the glow can't be bought, can't be earned, can't be faked. It only comes from being in His presence.

So let me flip this personal. Do you make space to sit with God, or are you too busy hustling? Are you so consumed with leading others that you forgot to be led yourself? Are you running on fumes when God's presence is the fuel?

Don't get it twisted, I'm not saying you'll walk around with your face literally shining, but people should be able to say, "Yo, something's different about him." When you're leading a company, your employees should notice the patience and strength you carry. When you're in ministry, your people should feel the weight of God's presence on you, not just your personality. That's the glow.

And let's be real, the glow costs something. Moses had to climb the mountain. He had to sacrifice time. He had to be alone with God. The glow doesn't come cheap, but it's worth it. Because true leaders don't just direct people, they reflect God.

Handle That

- **Block a daily 20**. Twenty minutes with God before you touch your phone. Bible. Prayer. Silence. Non negotiable for 7 days.
- **Confess that thing**. Write the one thing dimming your glow. Confess it to God. If needed, confess to a trusted friend.
- **One secret serve**. Do one act of generosity this week that nobody knows about. Let your Father see in secret.

Set aside a chunk of time this week just for God. No phone. No distractions. Just sit, pray, read His Word, and be still. Then check yourself afterward, did your patience hit different? Did your words shift? Did people notice something you didn't? That's the glow at work.

Take Note

- When did I feel most "lit up" in God's presence, and what habits fed that season.
- Who in my life today reflects Jesus in a way that convicts and inspires me. What do they practice that I can adopt.
- Where do I sense God inviting me to slow down. What will I say no to so I can say yes to Him.
- If my team or family mirrored my current spiritual life, would they glow or grind.
- Do people see God's presence in me without me having to announce it?
- Am I chasing platforms more than I'm chasing His presence?
- What shines through me most; stress, ego, anger, or God's Spirit?

Take It to God

Father, thank You for the reminder that Your presence changes everything. Forgive me for the times I've been too busy to sit with You. Teach me to climb the mountain daily, to make space for Your presence in my life. Let Your glow shine through me, in my family, my work, my ministry, even in the darkest places. May people see You in me without me saying a word. I want the real glow, not a fake smile or a staged faith. I confess the things that dimmed my light. Clean my heart. Slow my pace. Draw me back to the place where I hear Your voice and carry Your presence. Fill me with Your Spirit so the fruit shows up in my face and in my choices. Make my life a signal that points people to Jesus. Restore my first love and let me shine for Your glory. **In Jesus Name, Amen.**

Falling On Your Face

"Then Moses and Aaron fell on their faces before all the assembly of the congregation of the Israelites." - (Numbers 14:5 AMP)

Life and Leadership Lesson

Boom! This right here is one of the most slept-on moves in leadership. Falling on your face. Most folks think leadership is about standing tall, chest out, giving orders, looking strong, having followers. But Moses flipped the script. Over and over, when things got crazy, he fell on his face.

Check the record:

- **Exodus 3:6** - At the burning bush, Moses hid his face and bowed because he realized he was standing on holy ground.

- **Exodus 32:9-14** - After the golden calf, God was ready to wipe out Israel. Moses fell before God and interceded for the people.
- **Numbers 12:13** - When Miriam got struck with leprosy, Moses cried out and basically hit his knees to plead for her healing.
- **Numbers 14:5** - The people were ready to fire him as leader, pick someone else, and head back to Egypt. Moses and Aaron? They fell on their faces before the whole crowd.
- **Exodus 34:8** - When God revealed His glory, Moses bowed low to the ground in worship.
- **Numbers 16:4** - When Korah and his crew tried to take over, Moses didn't fight back with fists. He fell on his face and let God handle it.

That's a pattern, bro. Falling on your face was Moses' go-to move. When he didn't know what to do, when people turned against him, when his back was against the wall, he went face down before God.

So what does it mean to fall on your face? It's surrender. It's saying, "God, this is bigger than me. I can't handle it, but You can." It's humility. It's worship. It's intercession. And it's leadership. Because real leaders don't always have the answers, but they know where to go to get them.

The crazy part? It ain't just Moses. **Abraham fell on his face when God made covenant with him (Genesis 17:3). Joshua fell on his face before the angel of the Lord (Joshua 5:14). David bowed with his face to the ground (1 Samuel 24:8).** Even Jesus fell on His face in the Garden of Gethsemane when He prayed, **"Not my will but Yours be done" (Matthew 26:39).**

So think about it, when's the last time you fell on your face? When you got that diagnosis? When the money ran out? When your team turned on you? When your family doubted you? Or do you just try to handle it in your own strength?

Now, this is a life and leadership lesson. Falling on your face ain't weakness, it's power. It's setting the example for your people. Imagine your crew seeing you hit the ground, not in defeat but in surrender to God. That's leadership. That's humility. That's strength.

Sometimes, the best move as a leader isn't standing tall but laying low. Let your people see where your help comes from. Let them know you ain't depending on your own muscle, your own hustle, or your own brainpower, you're depending on God.

Nah, falling on your face doesn't mean doing nothing. It means starting with God before you do anything. That's what separates leaders who burn out from leaders who keep going.

Handle That

This week, don't just pray sitting up or lying in bed. Take one situation that's heavy on you, get on the ground, and literally put your face down. Surrender it to God. Let your body match your heart.

Take Note

- What situations in my life have me stressed enough to fall on my face?
- Do I see falling on my face as weakness or strength?
- How can I model humility and surrender to the people I lead?
- Am I leading from my own strength or showing others what it means to lean on God?

Take It to God

Father, teach me the power of falling on my face. Forgive me for thinking leadership always means standing tall in my own strength. Remind me that true leadership starts in surrender. When the weight feels too heavy, let me hit the ground and lay it before You. Help me lead by example so others know where to turn when life gets crazy. **In Jesus' Name, Amen.**

Chapter 24

Look Up or Die Tryin'

(When the Snakes Come Out)

"Then the people of Israel set out from Mount Hor, taking the road to the Red Sea to go around the land of Edom. But the people grew impatient with the long journey, and they began to speak against God and Moses. 'Why have you brought us out of Egypt to die here in the wilderness?' they complained. 'There is nothing to eat here and nothing to drink. And we hate this horrible manna!' So the Lord sent poisonous snakes among the people, and many were bitten and died. Then the people came to Moses and cried out, 'We have sinned by speaking against the Lord and against you. Pray that the Lord will take away the snakes.' So Moses prayed for the people. Then the Lord told him, 'Make a replica of a poisonous snake and attach it to a pole. All who are bitten will live if they simply look at it!' So Moses made a snake out of bronze and attached it to a pole. Then anyone who was bitten by a snake could look at the bronze snake and be healed."

- (Numbers 21:4-9 NLT)

Life and Leadership Lesson

After all the miracles they've seen, they still decided to complain. That's crazy. The people were dying because of their own rebellion, and God gave them a simple instruction, look up and live. That's it. Not fight harder, not run faster, not hustle more, just look up. Imagine being in the middle of the desert with snakes crawling out of the ground, biting everybody around you. People dying left and right. Fear everywhere. What's the solution? God says, "Look up." That's crazy simple, right? Look up at the bronze snake on the pole.

This is wild. God had just been feeding them, guiding them, protecting them, but the people still found something to complain about. Instead of gratitude, they chose grumbling. Instead of trusting, they started whining. And that ungrateful spirit brought snakes up in their camp and some knuckleheads still refused.

As weird as this story might be, all they had to do was look and believe. Simply just an exercise of faith. I'm sure God could have easily just removed the snakes but instead left them and taught them a lesson of having faith and looking to God for salvation. Think about it, when we are going through our problems and we cry out to Him, He doesn't remove our problems, He strengthens our faith with a lesson in the middle of it. Boom!

Now think about your life. How many times have you been bit? Maybe not by snakes, but by betrayal, addiction, anger, lust, pride, depression, or failure. The venom spreads quickly. You feel it eating at your confidence, your relationships, your leadership. You feel like time is running out.

And here's the word, the only way out is to look up. Stop trying to fix everything on your own. Stop pretending you got it all handled. Leaders, inmates, hustlers, business owners, pastors, this is for all of us. You can grind, you can plan, you can flex, but at the end of the day, you need God to save you.

This story points straight to Jesus. **John 3:14-15** says, ***"As Moses lifted up the serpent in the wilderness, so must the Son of Man be lifted up, that whoever believes in him may have eternal life."*** That means your survival depends on where you're looking. Are your eyes on the bite, or on the One who can heal you?

Let's be real, sometimes we focus too much on the poison. We replay the betrayal, the loss, the criticism in our mind. We stare at the wound instead of the Healer. That's like staring at the snake bite while the antidote is right in front of you.

David had to look up when he was surrounded by enemies and depression was choking him out. That's why he said, ***"I lift up my eyes to the hills. From where does my help come? My help comes from the Lord"*** (**Psalm 121:1-2**). Peter learned this when he was walking on water. As long as his eyes were on Jesus, he stayed above the waves. The second he looked at the storm, that dude sank (**Matthew 14:29-30**).

So here's the question, what are you looking at right now? The problem or the Provider? The bite or the blessing? The failure or the Father?

Leadership is not about being perfect. It's about knowing where to look when life gets wild. It's about setting the example for those following you. If the people you lead see you looking up, they'll learn to do the same.

This story ain't just about snakes. It's about life. It's about leadership. It's about how we respond when life bites us. When betrayal, addiction, depression, loss, or failure sink their teeth into you, what do you do? Do you stare at the wound, keep focusing on the pain, keep replaying the hurt? Or do you look up to the One who brings healing?

Leaders gotta get this. Because people are watching how you handle the bite. If you're a business owner, what do you do when your company hits a crisis? If you're a pastor, how do you lead when half your church walks out? If you're locked up, how do you act when you get the news that your appeal got denied? Snakes are coming at all of us. It's not about avoiding them. It's about where you look when they show up.

Let's be real, it ain't always easy to look up. Fear makes you freeze. Guilt makes you hide. Pride makes you think you can handle the venom on your own. But if you keep staring at your pain, you'll bleed out. Leadership means looking up first so you can point others to the source of healing.

Look at **Peter in Matthew 14:28-31**. He walked on water when his eyes were locked on Jesus, but the second he looked at the wind and waves, he sank. Same principle. Focus determines survival. Or think about **Stephen in Acts 7:55**. As they were stoning him to death, he wasn't staring at the crowd. He looked up and saw Jesus standing at the right hand of God. That's what gave him peace in the middle of pain.

So here's the real question:

- What bites are you carrying right now?
- Are you still staring at the scar, or are you looking up for healing?

- As a leader, are you teaching your people to look up or letting them die trying to fix themselves?

Crazy thing is, some people will rather die than look up. Pride will keep them stuck. Don't be *that* leader.

Let's be real, how do you react when things don't go your way? Do you thank God for what you *do* have, or do you complain about what you don't? Do you look back at Egypt like, "Man, maybe it was better there," and forgetting how miserable slavery really was?

This story ain't just about snakes in the wilderness. It's about how dangerous complaining can be. Complaining blinds you. It makes you miss the miracles right in front of you. It makes you forget what God already did for you. It shifts your focus from faith to fear, from God's provision to your problems.

Crazy, right? Complaining brought death, but looking up brought life. And that's the same today. Leaders, inmates, business owners, moms, pastors, your perspective will either poison you or save you.

So let me ask you: what's got you complaining right now? Is it your job? Your marriage? Your church? Your money? Your cell? What snakes are slithering through your camp because you won't stop grumbling?

Instead of focusing on what you don't have, look up. Look to Jesus. The more you complain, the more poison spreads. The more you worship, the more healing comes.

Paul wrote in **Philippians 2:14**, *"Do everything without grumbling or arguing."* That ain't easy, but it's a survival tactic. Complaining kills momentum, kills gratitude, kills vision. But gratitude shifts everything.

Handle That

- Write down the "snakes" in your life right now, addictions, failures, financial struggles, family issues. Be real about it.
- For each one, write a way you can shift your focus upward instead of staring at the bite.
- Pray for your crew, your family, your church, or your team. Teach them to look up when life bites.

This week, when you feel the venom of stress, rejection, or fear rising up in your veins, pause and shift your focus. Write down what you're looking at more, your problem or your God. Then decide to look up and hand it over to Him.

Take Note

- What's been my first reaction when I get "bitten", panic, anger, pride, or looking to God?
- Have I been showing others how to look up, or have I been too busy staring at my own wounds?
- Do I believe healing is really that simple?
- What bites from my past are still poisoning me today?
- Am I more focused on my wounds or on my Healer?
- Do the people I lead see me looking up when things go wrong?
- What would change in my leadership if I consistently shifted my focus to God?

Take It to God

Father, I admit I've been staring at the bite instead of looking at You. I've let pain, rejection, and stress poison my spirit. But today I choose to look up. Help me to keep my eyes fixed on You when life gets crazy. Make me a leader who shows others where to look, not by my words only but by my example. Heal me from the venom of my past, and let me walk in freedom. You've given us a way out when life bites us. Forgive me for the times I kept staring at my wounds instead of looking up to You. Teach me to keep my eyes fixed on Jesus, the One lifted up for my healing and salvation. Help me lead others by example, showing them that no matter what venom is running through their veins, there's always hope if we look to You. Keep me humble, keep me steady, and remind me that healing always starts by looking up. **In Jesus' Name, Amen.**

Chapter 25

Stand In The Gap

"But now, please forgive their sin, but if not, then blot me out of the book you have written." - (Exodus 32:32)

Life and Leadership Lesson

As I've been saying since the beginning, leadership is about standing up for others, I mean it literally, and Moses lived this. This wasn't a one-time thing when he prayed for Israel after the golden calf. From the very beginning, Moses was a stand-up guy.

Peep this:

- In **Exodus 2:11-12**, he saw a Hebrew slave getting beat down by an Egyptian. Instead of ignoring it, he stepped in. He couldn't just watch injustice go down and stay quiet. He stood on business.
- In **Exodus 2:16-17**, when shepherds tried to punk Jethro's daughters at the well, Moses jumped in again and defended them. He didn't even know them, he just couldn't sit back while someone got mistreated.

- In **Exodus 32:11-14**, after Israel worshipped the golden calf, God was ready to wipe them out. Moses stood in the gap and said, "Don't destroy them, Lord. What will the Egyptians say? Show them mercy." That's bold. He even reminded God of His own promises. Boom. That's wild.

- Then in **Exodus 32:32**, he takes it further. "If You won't forgive them, then erase me from Your book too." This dude was putting others first, even when it cost him.

You'll see this throughout Moses' whole *unlikely leadership* story. It's about standing up. Not for himself, but for others.

And he wasn't the only one.

- **Abraham** stood in the gap for Sodom in **Genesis 18**, pleading with God to spare the city if even ten righteous people were there.

- **David** stood up for Israel when Goliath mocked them in 1 **Samuel 17**. He didn't even go out there for himself, he went because nobody else would.

- **Esther** stood before the king in **Esther 4:16**, saying "If I perish, I perish," to save her people.

- **Jesus** stood up for a woman caught in adultery in **John 8**, shutting down the mob that wanted to stone her. Then He stood up for all of us on the cross, literally taking the hit we deserved.

Leaders stand up. Period.

So let me ask you this, who are you standing up for? Are you using your position, your voice, your influence for others, or just for yourself? If you're a CEO, are you standing up for your employees? If you're a father, are you standing up for your kids when the world tries to beat them down? If you're locked up, are you standing up for the guy in your unit who everybody clowns?

Jesus said in **Matthew 25:40**, *"Whatever you did for one of the least of these brothers and sisters of mine, you did for me."* That's the test. Leadership isn't about how high you climb. It's about who you bend down to lift up.

Crazy, right? The least of these are the real test of your leadership.

Handle That

Find one person around you who has no voice or no power, and stand up for them. It might be someone at work or someone in your neighborhood, someone in your cell block, or someone in your family. Don't just pray for them. Act.

Take Note

- Who has God put in my life that I need to stand up for?
- Am I willing to take a hit for someone else the way Moses did?
- Do I stand up when I see injustice, or do I stay quiet to protect myself?
- Am I leading for me, or for "the least of these"?

Take It to God

Father, thank You for leaders like Moses, David, Esther, and Jesus who stood up when others stayed silent. Teach me to be that kind of leader. Forgive me for the times I've stayed quiet when I should have spoken. Give me courage to use my voice, my influence, and my life for the ones who can't defend themselves. Help me lead not for myself, but for the least of these. **In Jesus' Name, Amen.**

Don't Allow Our Enemies to Talk Smack About Our God

"Why should the Egyptians say, 'It was with evil intent that he brought them out, to kill them in the mountains and to wipe them off the face of the earth'? Turn from your fierce anger; relent and do not bring disaster on your people."
- (Exodus 32:12)

Life and Leadership Lesson

Boom! Moses was bold. God was ready to wipe Israel clean after the golden calf fiasco, and Moses stepped in. Not because Israel deserved it, they didn't. Not because Moses was worried about himself, he wasn't. He did it because of God's name. Moses basically said, "Hold up, Lord, don't let the Egyptians clown You. Don't let them say You brought us out here just to kill us."

That's wild, but it shows you something: Moses was more concerned about God's reputation than his own. That's honor. That's leadership.

And let's be real, we live in a world full of haters, doubters, and skeptics. They're watching how you live, how you lead, how you react under pressure. If you claim God but your life doesn't line up, guess what? They're gonna talk smack about Him. Just like Paul said in **Romans 2:24** - ***"God's name is blasphemed among the Gentiles because of you."***

So ask yourself: are my actions honoring God's name, or giving people ammo to doubt Him?

Look at David. When Goliath stepped up, David didn't say, "You're disrespecting me." *He said, "You come against me with sword and spear, but I come against you in the name of the Lord Almighty" (1 Samuel 17:45).* David was defending God's honor.

Or check out Jesus in **John 17:4**, *"I have brought you glory on earth by finishing the work you gave me to do."* His whole mission was about the Father's glory.

Leaders, hear me. Whether you're running a business, pastoring a church, supervising a crew, raising a family, or sitting in a cell, you carry God's name with you. People are watching. Your wins and losses, your mistakes and victories, your public and private life, it all reflects back on Him.

The crazy part? Moses could've used that moment to level up. God literally said, "I'll destroy them and make you a great nation" (**Exodus 32:10**). Boom, imagine that, Moses' face on the billboard instead of Abraham's. But he said no. He valued God's name over his own legacy. That's humility. That's loyalty. That's real leadership.

So let me ask you: do you care more about building your own name, or protecting God's? Are you more worried about your brand, your followers, your respect, or about how people see Him through you?

Handle That

Think about one area where your actions might not be lining up with what you say you believe. Maybe it's how you deal with money, anger, sex, influence, or leadership. Make a move this week that shifts the focus back to honoring God's name.

Take Note

- When people look at my life, do they respect God more or doubt Him more?
- Am I more concerned about my reputation or God's?
- Do I make leadership decisions based on my own clout or on God's glory?
- How can I protect God's name in my home, my work, or my crew?**Take It to God**

Father, thank You for trusting me to carry Your name. Forgive me for the times I've lived in a way that gave haters a reason to doubt You. Teach me to be like Moses, ready to step up and defend Your honor above my own. Let my life, my leadership, and my choices reflect Your goodness. May people see You through me, not because I'm perfect, but because I'm Yours. **In Jesus' Name, Amen.**

Interceding for the
Ones Who Hurt You

"The Lord said to Moses, 'How long will these people treat me with contempt? How long will they refuse to believe in me, in spite of all the signs I have performed among them? ... I will strike them down with a plague and destroy them, but I will make you into a nation greater and stronger than they.' ... Moses said to the Lord, 'Then the Egyptians will hear about it! ... Now may the Lord's strength be displayed, just as you have declared: The Lord is slow to anger, abounding in love and forgiving sin and rebellion. ... In accordance with your great love, forgive the sin of these people.' The Lord replied, 'I have forgiven them, as you asked." - (Numbers 14:11-20)

Life and Leadership Lesson

Moses could've taken the deal. God was ready to wipe everybody out and start fresh with him. Most leaders would've jumped at that. Imagine God telling you, "I'll get rid of all the drama, all the backstabbers, all the doubters, and make you the guy." But Moses didn't bite. Instead, he falls on his face and intercedes for the very people who talked trash about him, doubted him, rejected him, and even threatened to stone him. That's leadership on another level.

Let's keep it real. How do you respond when the ones you've been praying for, betray you or turn their back? That's not easy. But Moses shows us that we're not just supposed to fight for the ones who cheer us, but also for the ones who hurt us.

This is where leadership gets tested. Anyone can love the ones who love them back. Jesus said it plain: ***"Love your enemies and pray for those who persecute you" (Matthew 5:44).*** That's a command, not a suggestion. And He lived it. On the cross, while the same crowd mocked Him, He said, ***"Father, forgive them, for they know not what they do" (Luke 23:34).***

Paul interceded for the churches that broke his heart. Think about Corinth, those folks questioned his authority, doubted his calling, and yet he still wrote letters pleading with them, correcting them, and pointing them back to Jesus (**2 Corinthians 2:4**). And as the rocks were bouncing off of Stephen, he prayed, ***"Lord, do not hold this sin against them" (Acts 7:60).*** He interceded for the people literally killing him. That's wild.

So let me ask you:

- Who do you need to intercede for right now, even though they've hurt you?

- Do you only pray for the people you vibe with, or do you pray for the ones who betrayed you?
- As a leader, can God trust you to stand in the gap for the ones who stab you in the back?

For my brothers locked up, maybe it's that family member who turned their back when you needed them most. Maybe it's the system that broke you down. But instead of staying bitter, can you intercede and ask God to move in their life?

For the CEO, the hustler, the pastor, maybe it's an employee who left your business wrong, a church member who spread lies, or a partner who back-stabbed you for a dollar. Are you willing to still pray for them? That's the mark of true leadership.

The life lesson here is about standing in the gap for people when they don't deserve it, when they don't say thank you, when they spit in your face. Because the truth is, that's exactly what Jesus did for us.

Imagine this, the people trash-talk you, disrespect you, reject you, and treat you like you're worthless. Then God says, "I'll wipe them out and start fresh with you." Most folks would be like, "Alright. Do it, Lord." But not Moses. He falls on his face and intercedes for them.

That right there is leadership and humility. That is what it looks like to love people even when they don't love you back. You carry the weight for others even when they don't deserve it. You bring their names before God when they don't even pray for themselves.

Ask yourself: when was the last time you prayed for the ones who hurt you? Would you stand in the gap for the people who lied on you, betrayed you, or walked out on you? That's next-level. That's the kind of leadership God honors.

Moses wasn't the only one.

- **Abraham** interceded for Sodom, asking God to spare the city if there were even ten righteous people there (**Genesis 18:22-32**).
- **Job** prayed for his friends even after they accused him (**Job 42:10**).
- **Jesus** on the cross said, *"Father, forgive them, for they know not what they do"* (**Luke 23:34**). Boom, that's the ultimate intercession.
- **Paul** prayed for his people Israel, saying he'd even be cut off if it meant they could be saved (**Romans 9:3**).

Let's make it personal. Who hurt you? Who backstabbed you? Who doubted you? Who said you'd never make it, never change, never lead? You gonna hold that grudge, or you gonna stand in the gap like Moses did?

It's about saying, "God, don't take them out. Show them mercy. Forgive them like You forgave me." That's real power. That's what fathers do for their kids, what pastors do for their flock, what business owners do for their teams, what prayer warriors do for their families.

And here's what's wild, when you intercede, it changes you too. It breaks bitterness. It heals wounds. It frees your heart from the poison of revenge. Forgiveness isn't letting them off the hook, it's letting God handle it His way.

So let me ask you, are you carrying grudges? Are you begging God for all those people or just for yourself?

Handle That

Write down the name of someone who hurt you, maybe a family member, a friend, a boss, a cellmate, a church member, a co-worker, an ex. Instead of plotting payback, take five minutes today and pray for them. Ask God to bless them, forgive them, and show them mercy.

Take Note

- Who's the hardest person in my life to pray for right now? And why?
- Do I want revenge more than I want God's mercy?
- How would my leadership shift if I interceded more and complained less?
- Am I willing to stand in the gap for others like Moses, even if it costs me?

Take It to God

Father, thank You for interceding for me through Jesus when I didn't deserve it. Teach me to be a leader who stands in the gap for others, even the ones who hurt me. Break the spirit of bitterness in me and replace it with compassion. Remind me that intercession is not weakness, it's strength. Give me the courage to pray for my enemies and the humility to plead for mercy over those who fail me. Lord, this one's tough. It's easy to pray for the people who love me, but it's hard to pray for the ones who hurt me. Teach me to be a leader who stands in the gap even for my enemies. Help me to forgive and to carry others in prayer even when they don't deserve it. Make me a leader who loves beyond the pain. **In Jesus' Name, Amen.**

Chapter 26

Changing Your Perspective

"We even saw giants there, the descendants of Anak. Next to them we felt like grasshoppers, and that's what they thought, too!"
- (Numbers 13:33 NLT)

Life and Leadership Lesson

The spies saw giants in the land, but the real problem wasn't the giants, it was how they saw themselves. They said, "We seemed like grasshoppers in our own eyes." Crazy. They disqualified themselves before the fight even started. Boom! That's wild. Imagine being right at the edge of the Promised Land, everything God told you was about to pop off, and instead of running in with faith, these dudes said, "We felt like grasshoppers." That right there is perspective. How you see yourself will determine how you step into your assignment.

Let me ask you, how do you see yourself? When you look at your situation, do you see yourself as the underdog, the nobody, the one that can't? Or do you see yourself through God's eyes, chosen, equipped, and backed by heaven? Let's keep it real. Sometimes the biggest battle ain't the giant in front of you. It's the giant in your mind. It's the story you've been telling yourself. "I'm too small. I'm too broken. I'm not qualified."

Sound familiar? Street dudes know this. You're trying to rebuild your life, but you keep saying, "Nah, I'll never make it out the system." Entrepreneurs know this, you're trying to launch that business, but you're thinking, "I'm just one person. How can I compete with the big dogs?" Pastors feel it too. You're leading a flock but you're looking at every other church's highlight reel thinking you're not enough.

Perspective is everything. Two guys (Joshua and Caleb) saw the same giants and said, "We can take them, God is with us." The other ten saw the giants and said, "Nah, we're done, we're too small." Same land, same enemies, different eyes. Leaders see differently. Different perspectives. Caleb said, ***Let's go right now. We can take them" (Numbers 13:30).*** Perspective is the difference between hesitation and action. Between faith and fear. Between quitting and stepping forward.

Just gotta see it through different lenses. Buried, or planted? It's all in how you look at it! Do you see yourself buried in your current situation or are you planted there by God to bloom and teach others to bloom where they are planted?

Sometimes we need to take a step back from certain situations and look from another perspective. All we need to do is reframe the situation and change the way we look at things.

You can ask this question and get so many different answers. So, I asked my daughter Gianni that question that many people ask about Adolf Hitler. "Would you have him killed as a youngster if you knew he was going to become what he became?"

Her response was so different and with a completely fresh perspective. She didn't mention any violence towards him, no secret assassination plot or special forces hunting him down. Instead she just looked at things differently and said, "I would go back and change his surroundings, soften up how his teachers spoke to him about his art, have people speak life into him and give him positive affirmations instead of the negativity he was given."

I never thought about it like that. My 19 year-old daughter had a totally different perspective that helped me see how our surroundings and what we are encouraged to grow in will deeply affect our mindset.

Now think about your life. Are you looking at your prison time as wasted years, or as a season God can use to reshape you, sharpen you, and set you up for purpose? Are you looking at your business struggles as proof you should quit, or as training ground for a bigger breakthrough? Are you looking at your family drama as hopeless, or as the very place God wants to show His glory?

What are the giants around you right now that make you feel like a grasshopper? I'm not saying these type of giants are real today. Bills are real. Court dates are real. Sickness is real. Betrayal is real. But sometimes the size of the giant ain't the real problem, it's the size of your faith. You can stare at the obstacle until it looks ten times bigger than it is. Or you can stare at God until your faith looks ten times stronger than you thought it was.

David had that same perspective shift. Everybody saw Goliath as a giant too big to fight. David saw him as a giant too big to miss. That's different eyes. Paul did it too, sitting in prison, he could've said, "This is the end." Instead he wrote, "What has happened to me has really served to advance the gospel" (**Philippians 1:12**). He saw his chains as a platform, not a problem.

So I'll ask you again: what do you see? Do you see yourself as a grasshopper or a giant killer? Do you see your current struggle as the end, or as the setup? Do you see that rejection as failure, or as God's redirection?

Leaders don't just accept the first perspective handed to them. They ask, "What's another way to see this?" That's what separates winners from quitters, builders from complainers, faithful leaders from fearful ones.

What about you? Are you looking at your challenges through the lens of your limits or through the lens of God's promises? Do you see prison time as wasted years or as training ground? Do you see that financial struggle as the end of your story or the place where God builds your faith muscles? Do you see rejection as a closed door or as God redirecting you to better?

Scripture drops example after example.

- **David** saw Goliath and said, ***"Who is this uncircumcised Philistine defying the armies of the living God?" (1 Samuel 17:26)***. He didn't see a giant problem, he saw a chance for God to show off.
- **Joseph** looked back at betrayal and prison and said, "***You meant it for evil, but God meant it for good" (Genesis 50:20)***. Perspective turned pain into purpose.
- **Paul** sat in chains and wrote, ***"What has happened to me has actually advanced the gospel" (Philippians 1:12-14)***. He didn't see prison as punishment, he saw it as a pulpit.

Crazy, right? Your perspective can either paralyze you or propel you.

Leaders, listen. If you see yourself as a grasshopper, people around you will start seeing you that way too. But when you carry faith, it's contagious. Your crew, your team, your congregation, your family, they will catch your courage. Joshua and Caleb had a different spirit, and decades later, Joshua was the one leading the people in.

Ask yourself:

- What giants am I exaggerating right now because of fear?
- What promises of God am I downplaying because I see myself too small?
- Am I speaking like the ten spies, spreading doubt, or like Joshua and Caleb, spreading faith?

This ain't just positive thinking. It's not fake hype. It's about aligning how you see yourself with how God already sees you. **Romans 8:37** says you're more than a conqueror. **1 Peter 2:9** says you're chosen, royal, and set apart. **2 Timothy 1:7** says you've been given a spirit of power, love, and a sound mind.

For my people behind bars, your situation might look like a giant. But how are you gonna see it? Is it only punishment, or can it be preparation? For my hustlers in business, when you look at competition, do you shrink back or do you say, "God gave me this lane, and I'm gonna own it"? For my pastors, are you comparing your church to others, or are you faithful with the sheep in your hand like David with his few?

Here's the deal. Grasshopper thinking will keep you wandering when giant-slayer faith will move you forward.

Handle That

Take one challenge you're facing right now: maybe financial, personal, or spiritual. Write down how you've been seeing it. Then flip it and write down how God might see it. Look at it through His promises, not your fears.

Take Note

- Where in my life do I keep seeing myself as small?
- Who around me needs me to stop talking like a grasshopper and start talking like Caleb?
- How have I seen God flip my perspective in the past, and what did it do for my leadership?
- Where am I seeing myself as a grasshopper when God calls me more?
- How have my fears been shaping my perspective?

Take It to God

Father, open my eyes to see things the way You see them. Forgive me for the times I let fear shrink me down to a grasshopper. Teach me to see giants as opportunities, not obstacles. Change my perspective in prison, in business, in family, and in leadership. Help me lead with faith, not fear, and to remind others that with You nothing is too big. I admit I've seen myself too small at times. I've let fear, shame, and comparison make me feel like a grasshopper. But I know You've called me more than a conqueror. Change how I see myself. Change how I see my giants. Give me the faith of Joshua and Caleb to say, "We can take the land." Let my perspective reflect Your promises, not my fears. Help me lead with courage so others can catch it too. **In Jesus' Name, Amen.**

Chapter 27

When You Take Your Eyes Off God

"Take the staff, and assemble the congregation, you and Aaron your brother, and tell the rock before their eyes to yield its water. So you shall bring water out of the rock for them and give drink to the congregation and their cattle. And Moses took the staff from before the Lord, as he commanded him. Then Moses and Aaron gathered the assembly together before the rock, and he said to them, 'Hear now, you rebels: shall we bring water for you out of this rock?' And Moses lifted up his hand and struck the rock with his staff twice, and water came out abundantly, and the congregation drank, and their livestock. And the Lord said to Moses and Aaron, 'Because you did not believe in me, to uphold me as holy in the eyes of the people of Israel, therefore you shall not bring this assembly into the land that I have given them." - (Numbers 20:8-12 ESV)

Life and Leadership Lesson

One moment of losing focus cost Moses the promised land. Think about that, after all the miracles, all the leadership, all the sacrifices, he let anger and distraction take his eyes off God's instructions. He struck the rock when God told him to speak to it. And just like that, consequences.

Moses had been leading, interceding, sacrificing, putting up with complaints for years, but in this moment, he slipped. Instead of doing exactly what God told him to do, "speak to the rock", he struck it in anger. God still provided the water, but Moses lost out on stepping into the Promised Land. That right there shows us how dangerous it is when leaders take their eyes off God, even for a second.

Keep it real. How many of us have been in Moses' shoes? Stressed out. Frustrated. Mad at people we're leading. Tired of the constant weight. And then we act out of emotion instead of obedience. We stop listening and start reacting. We stop trusting and start performing. Leaders, you can't afford to let pressure push you out of God's presence.

Ask yourself, where are you striking rocks when God told you to speak? Maybe in business, you're forcing deals to happen instead of trusting God's timing. Maybe in ministry, you're putting on a show instead of simply obeying. Maybe in your family, you're snapping in anger instead of letting patience do its work. Moses let his frustration with the people shift his focus. He took his eyes off God and put them on the problem. And it cost him. It's happened to me.

How many times have you taken your eyes off God because the people, the pressure, or your own emotions pushed you into reacting? How many times have you let busyness, stress, or distractions pull you out of alignment with what God told you to do? Leaders deal with this every day. A CEO gets so caught up in the grind that prayer becomes an afterthought. A pastor gets so busy doing ministry that they forget to sit with God. A father gets distracted by providing that he forgets to be present. Even someone locked up can lose focus, getting caught up in prison politics instead of the purpose God's trying to birth in them. Distractions are everywhere.

Distractions don't always look evil either. Sometimes they look like good things. Ministry, business, serving others, those are all good, but if they keep us from obeying God exactly how He said, they're still distractions. The enemy don't always need to destroy you, he just needs to distract you long enough to keep you from the full promise.

This ain't just a Moses thing either. Remember **Peter**? When he stepped out of the boat and started walking on water, he was solid while his eyes were on Jesus. But the second he noticed the wind and the waves, he started sinking **(Matthew 14:28-31)**. Same water. Same Jesus. Different focus. That whole story was about focusing and keeping your eyes on Jesus. Or think of **Samson**. God gave him power, but he kept fixing his eyes on Delilah instead of on his calling **(Judges 16:4-21)**. Lost it all because of distraction. **Colossians 3:2** says, **"Set your minds on things above, not on earthly things."** Why? Because whatever has your eyes will guide your steps.

Now think about this, what's got your eyes right now? Is it money, success, stress, fear, or the haters? Or is it God? If Moses could get distracted after hearing God's voice audibly and seeing miracles with his own eyes, bro, don't think we can't slip up too.

Leadership means learning to silence the noise and keep your focus locked on the One who called you. It means slowing down enough to hear His voice before reacting. It means choosing obedience even when pressure makes you want to pop off.

How about us? What are you looking at? Is it the storm, the stress, the critics, the haters? Or is it God? Leaders get distracted. Hustlers get distracted. Pastors get distracted. Inmates sitting in their cell can get distracted by the noise of the tier instead of the whisper of God. Distraction will always cost you more than obedience.

But here's the hope: even when Moses messed up, God still gave the people water. That shows His grace. But it also shows His standard. Leadership is weighty. If God trusted you with influence, you can't just do things your way when it gets hard. **Hebrews 12:2** says, **"We do this by keeping our eyes on Jesus, the champion who initiates and perfects our faith."** That's the only way to finish well.

So let me ask you:

- Where in your life are you striking when you should be speaking?
- What distractions keep pulling your eyes off God?
- How are you leading under pressure? With obedience or frustration?

This ain't about being perfect. It's about being faithful. It's about learning from Moses' mistake and choosing to trust God fully in the moments where your emotions want to take over. So let me ask you, are you leading from a place of focus or frustration? Are you carrying out God's instructions or your own reactions? Are you striking rocks in anger instead of speaking to them in faith?

Handle That

- Identify one area where you've been doing things your way instead of God's way. Write it down. Pray over it. Decide to shift your focus back.

- Ask a trusted brother, sister, or mentor to check you when you're leading out of frustration instead of obedience.
- Practice pausing before reacting. When pressure hits, stop and ask, "God, how do You want me to handle this?"

Take Note

- Am I more focused on the problem than the presence of God?
- What situations have I tried to control instead of surrendering?
- Where have I seen God's grace cover me even when I slipped up?

Take It to God

Father, I don't want to lead out of anger, fear, or frustration. I don't want to take my eyes off You and miss the blessing You've promised. Teach me to trust You enough to obey exactly what You say, even when the pressure is heavy. Help me to focus on You when distractions come. Keep me humble, keep me patient, and keep me obedient. I don't want to just get water from the rock, I want to walk into the promises You have for me. Forgive me for the times I've let distractions, pressure, or anger pull my eyes off You. Help me to stay focused on Your voice and Your Word above the noise. Teach me to lead out of obedience, not frustration. Keep me from striking the rock when You called me to speak to it. Let my eyes stay fixed on You so my leadership reflects Your holiness. **In Jesus' Name, Amen.**

Chapter 28

Oh Lord, Please Don't

Let Me Be Misunderstood

"That night all the members of the community raised their voices and wept aloud. All the Israelites grumbled against Moses and Aaron, and the whole assembly said to them, 'If only we had died in Egypt! Or in this wilderness! Why is the Lord bringing us to this land only to let us fall by the sword? Our wives and children will be taken as plunder. Wouldn't it be better for us to go back to Egypt?' And they said to each other, 'We should choose a leader and go back to Egypt.'"
- (Numbers 14:1-4)

Life and Leadership Lesson

One of the hardest things as a leader is being misunderstood. Moses gave his life for these people. He led them out of slavery, stood in front of Pharaoh, dealt with their complaints, prayed for their survival, and what did they do? They turned around and said, "Let's get a new leader and go back to Egypt." Boom. That's wild.

Think about it. After everything you pour out, people can flip on you in a second. That's what happened to Moses. And if you've ever led anything; a family, a crew, a church, a business, even a movement on the block, you know what it feels like to have people doubt you, question you, or completely misread your heart.

But here's the lesson: being misunderstood is part of leadership. People don't always see what you see. They don't always know what you know. They don't always value what you're sacrificing for them. Jesus Himself was misunderstood. His own family thought He was crazy (**Mark 3:21**). The Pharisees thought He was a threat to their system. The crowds wanted Him for miracles but turned on Him when He didn't fit their expectations. If Jesus was misunderstood, what makes you think you won't be?

Leaders, the weight of misunderstanding can crush you if you don't handle it right. The people in Numbers 14 straight up said they'd rather die than follow Moses anymore. That's cold. That's betrayal. But notice what Moses did. He didn't clap back. He didn't defend himself on social media. He didn't rally a new fan base. He fell on his face before God (**Numbers 14:5**).

That's the move right there. When you're misunderstood, the first place you go isn't people, it's God. Because here's the truth: when people don't get you, God still does.

So let me ask you: how do you respond when people misunderstand your vision, your heart, your leadership? Do you get defensive? Do you shut down? Do you quit? Or do you hit your knees and let God fight your battles?

Moses wasn't the only one. Joseph was misunderstood by his brothers, who thought his dreams were arrogance (**Genesis 37:8**). David was misunderstood by his brother Eliab when he showed up at the battlefield (**1 Samuel 17:28**). Paul was misunderstood and even abandoned by his own people (**2 Timothy 4:16**).

Misunderstanding is the tax of leadership. If you can't handle being misunderstood, you won't last long leading. But if you can take it to God, He'll use it to refine you instead of break you.

Here's the wildest part, sometimes being misunderstood is actually confirmation that you're walking in your calling. If everybody understood you, you probably wouldn't be doing anything significant. Vision always looks crazy until it comes to pass.

So what's your Egypt? What's that thing people keep saying you should go back to? What dream, business, ministry, or calling are they clowning because they don't get it? Are you willing to keep going anyway?

Leaders, never let misunderstanding drive you back to Egypt. God didn't bring you this far just to take you back where you started.

Handle That

Write down one time you were misunderstood in leadership, by family, coworkers, your church, or even friends. Instead of holding bitterness, pray over that moment. Ask God to show you how He was shaping you through it.

Take Note

- Who has misunderstood my calling or leadership?
- How do I usually react, defensiveness, silence, or prayer?
- Am I tempted to go "back to Egypt" just because people don't understand me?
- Do I believe God sees me clearly even when others don't?

Take It to God

Father, thank You that You see me and know me even when others misunderstand me. Forgive me for the times I let people's opinions stop me from walking in my calling. Teach me to respond like Moses, on my face before You, not fighting for my own reputation. Help me lead with grace, patience, and boldness even when I'm not understood. Keep me focused on where You're taking me, not where people want me to go back to. **In Jesus' Name, Amen.**

When They Don't Believe

"They said, 'May the Lord look on you and judge you! You have made us obnoxious to Pharaoh and his officials and have put a sword in their hand to kill us." - (Exodus 5:21)

Life and Leadership Lesson

Moses finally does what God told him. He goes back to Egypt, walks into Pharaoh's court, and says the famous line: ***"Let my people go."*** That should've been his big leadership moment, right? You'd think the people would've cheered him on. But nah. Instead of celebrating, the Israelites turned on him. They said, *"Bro, you just made things worse. Now Pharaoh hates us even more. May God judge you for this."*

Imagine that. Moses is literally risking his life to lead them, and the very people he's trying to save are doubting him, blaming him, and talking trash. That's leadership. Sometimes the people you're leading will not believe in you.

Let's be real, have you felt that before? You step out to do something you feel called to, and instead of applause, you get hate. You try to lead your family different, and they laugh at you. You start that business or ministry, and people roll their eyes like, *"Who do you think you are?"* You put your vision out, and instead of support, you get doubters, critics, or silence.

That hurts. Especially when it comes from your own people. Your own circle. The ones you thought would have your back.

But here's the thing: leadership means moving even when they don't believe. Moses had to learn that his assignment didn't depend on their approval. His calling came from God, not from the people. Same for you.

The truth is, there will always be doubters. People who can't see what God showed you. People who are too scared to leave Egypt themselves, so they project their fear on you. People who'd rather stay in chains than risk the unknown, and when you try to lead them out, they'll fight you.

So what do you do? Do you quit? Do you shrink back and say, *"Maybe they're right, maybe I'm not the one"*? Or do you keep walking in faith, knowing that obedience matters more than popularity?

Think about it. Jesus faced the same thing. He healed, loved, and preached truth, and His own people rejected Him. Leaders aren't validated by applause. They're validated by obedience.

So ask yourself, whose voice are you letting define your steps? The crowd's, or God's? Are you gonna let the noise of people's doubt paralyze you, or are you gonna keep walking toward your Red Sea moment? If I would have let the "people doubt" paralyze me then I would have never written this book. It's proof that you can do it too!

Handle That

List three times in your life where people doubted you. Write them down, but instead of letting them haunt you, declare over each one: *"God's call is bigger than their doubt."*

Take Note

- Who in your life has doubted or dismissed what God's called you to do?
- How did it affect the way you lead or move?
- What would change if you stopped needing their approval and started trusting only God's voice?

Take It to God

Father, I know what it feels like to be doubted, rejected, and even blamed when I'm just trying to follow You. Sometimes it hurts so deep that I want to quit. But remind me that my calling doesn't come from people, it comes from You. Give me strength to keep leading even when others don't believe. Teach me to stay faithful to the vision You gave me, not the opinions of the crowd. Help me lead with courage, even if I have to lead alone. **In Jesus' Name, Amen.**

Chapter 29

We All Got Issues

"When Moses approached the camp and saw the calf and the dancing, his anger burned and he threw the tablets out of his hands, breaking them to pieces at the foot of the mountain." - (Exodus 32:19)

"Then Moses raised his arm and struck the rock twice with his staff. Water gushed out, and the community and their livestock drank." - (Numbers 20:11)

"Better a patient person than a warrior, one with self-control than one who takes a city." - (Proverbs 16:32)

"Because human anger does not produce the righteousness that God desires." - (James 1:20)

Life and Leadership Lesson

For real though, Moses had some crazy anger issues. And not like small temper tantrums. This dude shattered the very tablets God Himself carved out. Wild right? Later, when God told him to speak to the rock, Moses let frustration get the best of him and struck it instead. That moment cost him the Promised Land.

Here's the truth, you can be called, anointed, chosen, and still have issues. We all got them. For some it's anger, for others it's pride, lust, greed, addiction, insecurity. What's yours?

I know mine. For some of us, anger was survival. You couldn't show weakness, couldn't let anyone punk you. Anger was your shield. It gave you respect. But in leadership, in family, in business, in faith, anger unchecked will wreck you.

Leaders, hear me. We cannot lead in anger. You might get temporary results by barking orders, snapping on people, or controlling with fear, but it destroys trust, relationships, and credibility. Proverbs says it's better to control yourself than to conquer a city. That's deep. Because most of us want to conquer, build, win, but the real flex is self-control.

And let's be real, some of us are losing more battles to our own emotions than to any enemy outside. You don't need Pharaoh to stop you. Sometimes it's your own temper, your own mouth, your own lack of patience.

But here's the good news: meekness is not weakness. Meekness is power under control. It's strength that's surrendered to God. Imagine how much more effective your leadership, your business, your ministry would be if you didn't keep blowing up, but instead led with peace and patience.

Here's something to ask yourself, how are you mismanaging your emotions? Are you still snapping at your spouse? Losing it at work? Cursing out the homie? Throwing things when stress piles up? Do you let frustration get the best of you? Are you bringing all this to The Lord?

Moses still led millions. He still parted the Red Sea. He still spoke face-to-face with God. But his anger kept him from walking into the very promise he lived for. Don't let anger rob you of your destiny. Let God work on you before it costs you something you can't afford to lose.

Handle That

Next time you feel that fire rising inside, pause. Breathe. Pray. Ask God, "Is this my battle to fight or Yours?" Write down three triggers that set you off, then come up with one new response for each. Don't just pray about it, apply it!

Take Note

- What are your triggers? What sets you off fast?
- How has anger already cost you in relationships, opportunities, or credibility?
- What would it look like for you to channel that same energy into patience, wisdom, and leadership?

Take It to God

Father, You know my issues. You know my temper, my frustration, the times I've let my emotions run wild. Forgive me for the damage I've done leading in anger. Teach me patience, self-control, and meekness. Remind me that true strength is found in surrendering to You, not flexing on others. Shape me into a leader who reflects Your peace, even when everything around me is chaotic. **In Jesus' Name, Amen.**

You're Not Exempt From the Drama

"But Zipporah took a flint knife, cut off her son's foreskin and touched Moses' feet with it. 'Surely you are a bridegroom of blood to me,' she said. So the Lord let him alone." - (Exodus 4:25-26)

Life and Leadership Lesson

This scripture is wild. It hits so close to home for me. God just got done speaking to Moses, calling him to deliver Israel, showing him miracles, backing him up. Moses is on his way to the biggest assignment of his life, and boom, drama breaks out at home. His wife Zipporah snaps on him and steps in with an attitude that probably shook the whole tent.

That's the part those in leadership forget, you're not exempt from the drama at home. You can be God's chosen, you can be His friend, you can be called to the nations, and still have arguments in your marriage. Still have friction with your kids. Still deal with family drama that makes you wonder, *"God, how am I supposed to lead Your people when I can't even keep peace in my house?"*

Let's keep it real. You could be respected in your community, running your business, pastoring a church, mentoring young dudes in the neighborhood, making moves that look strong in public, but if your family is falling apart in private, something's off. You can't be a success in public and a failure at home. That ain't leadership.

I'll be real with you: this is one of those areas I know too well. I know I could have done better as a husband and as a father. I know I've messed up, and I'm still working on it. Leading a family is not easy. It'll humble you faster than any pulpit, paycheck, or platform.

Your home is your first ministry. Before you lead crowds, before you lead employees, before you lead a congregation, you're called to lead your family. That doesn't mean you won't have drama, it means you fight to stay present in it. You learn to listen more, serve more, apologize quicker, and pray harder.

We may be the head of the house, but like they say, the wife is the neck that turns it. Don't act like you don't know. A house divided can't stand, and sometimes the greatest test of your leadership isn't out there, it's right under your roof.

Ask yourself this, where have you been slacking at home? Have you been so caught up chasing dreams, money, ministry, or even purpose that you've neglected your spouse, your kids, or your family? Have you let the drama get louder than your leadership? Lord knows I'm guilty of all that!

God never promised you wouldn't face conflict at home. He promised He'd be with you through it. And the same God that gives you wisdom to lead people will give you wisdom to lead your family, if you humble yourself and ask Him.

Handle That

Don't just lead in public. Go home and lead in private. Pick one area of your home life that needs your attention right now - your marriage, your kids, or even your personal character, and start investing there first.

Take Note

- What's one area in your family life you know you've been neglecting?
- How has the pressure of leadership outside the home affected your leadership inside the home?
- What's one step you can take today to be more present and intentional with your family?

Take It to God

Father, thank You for reminding me that my family is my first ministry. Forgive me for the times I've been more focused on leading outside than leading at home. I admit I've failed in some areas, but I don't want to keep failing. Give me patience, humility, and wisdom to love and serve my family well. Teach me to lead at home with the same passion I lead in public. Heal the areas I've broken and show me how to make things right. **In Jesus' Name, Amen.**

Chapter 30

I Thought I Had Favor?

"Moses said to the Lord, 'Why have you dealt ill with your servant? And why have I not found favor in your sight, that you lay the burden of all this people on me? Did I conceive all this people? Did I give them birth, that you should say to me, 'Carry them in your bosom, as a nurse carries a nursing child,' to the land that you swore to give their fathers?" - (Numbers 11:11-12 ESV)

Life and Leadership Lesson

Crazy. Even Moses, the man chosen to lead millions, had a moment where he felt played. He straight up told God, "Why are You doing me like this? I thought I had favor. Why You putting all this weight on me?" That's wild, because it's the same question some in leadership today ask when the load gets too heavy. Like, "God, I thought I had favor, so why does it feel like everything is on my back?" Moses was tired, and straight up overwhelmed. He thought favor meant life was supposed to get easier. But instead, the weight of leadership had him questioning if God even cared.

Now check it. Moses wasn't just leading a few people. He was carrying a whole nation that complained, doubted, and wanted to go back to Egypt every other day. Imagine being the one responsible for folks who keep turning on you. Sounds like being a CEO with a team that won't buy into the vision. Or like being locked up and trying to lead a group of men who don't trust anybody. Or being a dad in a house where it feels like nobody listens. You ever feel like that?

Here's the deal favor doesn't mean the absence of pressure. Favor means you're chosen to carry it. Look at Jesus in the Garden of Gethsemane. He was favored, but He still sweat drops of blood because of the weight He carried (**Luke 22:44**). Look at Joseph. He was favored with dreams, but that favor took him through a pit, slavery, and prison before the palace (**Genesis 37-41**). Look at Paul. Highly favored by God, yet shipwrecked, beaten, and thrown in prison (**2 Corinthians 11:23–28**).

Moses wasn't wrong for being real with God. Leaders need that. He vented, but notice what he did, he took it to God. That's the leadership lesson. The danger is when you hold it in and let it eat you alive. Leaders on the street, in the office, in the pulpit, in the cell, we all get worn down. The difference is, do you complain to people, or do you cry out to God?

And peep this: God didn't leave Moses hanging. Later in this same chapter, God gave him help by sharing the Spirit with 70 elders (**Numbers 11:16-17**). That's God saying, "You don't have to carry this weight alone." Crazy, right? Sometimes we think favor means "God take the load off," but often it means "God sends people to help you carry it." Notice what God did right after Moses snapped. He didn't curse him, He gave him help. Seventy others got the Spirit that was on Moses. We aren't meant to do it all solo. Are you willing to admit when it's too heavy and let God provide you with a team?

Favor is not about things being easy. Favor is about being trusted by God with responsibility. Favor is heavy sometimes, but it's worth it because it means God picked you for the assignment.

Maybe you thought starting that business meant blessings would overflow, but now you're drowning in bills. Maybe you thought being faithful in ministry meant peace, but instead you're dealing with drama in the pews. Maybe you thought raising your kids God's way meant smooth sailing, but now they're wilding out. Or maybe you're locked up, trying to get your life right, and you're wondering why the weight feels even heavier behind bars.

Here's the thing, favor doesn't mean no problems. Favor doesn't mean no haters. Favor doesn't mean no pressure. Favor means God is with you in the middle of it all. Favor is the presence of God in your pain. Favor is what kept Moses from quitting even when the people drove him crazy. Favor is what kept Joseph alive in prison until his purpose popped off. Favor is what carried David from the sheep pen to the throne, even though Saul tried to kill him. Favor is what kept Paul writing letters while chained up. And favor is what made Jesus say, "Not my will, but Yours" even when the cross was staring Him down.

Handle That

Start looking at favor as evidence of God's trust in you. Write down the top three burdens you're carrying right now, then pray and ask God who He's already sent to help you carry them. Don't keep trying to play Superman.

Take Note

- What burdens am I trying to carry alone?

- Who has God already placed around me to help me lead?

- When I complain about the weight, am I forgetting that His Spirit gives strength?

- How has God shown me I am favored even when I feel overwhelmed?

Take It to God

Father, thank You for showing me that favor doesn't mean easy. Forgive me for the times I've complained and questioned you, asking "why me" instead of trusting You. Teach me to see favor as Your presence in the pressure. Help me recognize the people You've placed in my life to help carry the load. Give me strength to keep leading, even when I feel like giving up. Show me the people You've placed in my life to help, and give me the humility to accept their support. Thank You for trusting me with this assignment, even when it feels like too much. **In Jesus' Name, Amen.**

Chapter 31

Second Chances Hit Different

When You've Been Counted Out

"The Lord said to Moses, 'Cut for yourself two tablets of stone like the first, and I will write on the tablets the words that were on the first tablets, which you broke. Be ready by the morning, and come up in the morning to Mount Sinai, and present yourself there to me on the top of the mountain." - *(Exodus 34:1-2 ESV)*

Life and Leadership Lesson

That's wild. Moses went full-on angry mode, smashed the tablets God Himself had written, and in that moment it looked like he ruined everything. Imagine the weight of that. God just gave him the law, the covenant, written by His own hand, and Moses destroyed it in a fit of rage. If anybody should have been disqualified right there, it was him.

But check how God moves. Instead of saying, "You blew it, you're done," God tells Moses, "Cut some new tablets and come back up the mountain. I'll rewrite what I already wrote." That's grace. That's redemption. That's the power of second chances.

Let me ask you straight up, how many times have you smashed what God put in your hands? Maybe you ruined a relationship, burned a bridge, or caused pain that can't be taken away? How many times have you blown it in anger, pride, addiction, or fear? How many times have you thought, "That's it, I'm done, God can't use me now"?

This story tells us leaders mess up too. You can love God, be called by Him, walk with Him, and still make mistakes. But the beauty is, failure doesn't have to be final. God is willing to renew and redeem if you're willing to humble yourself and climb back up the mountain.

The Bible is full of second chances:

- **Jonah** ran from God, but God sent the fish to give him another shot at Nineveh (**Jonah 3:1-2**)
- **Peter** denied Jesus three times, but Jesus restored him and told him, "Feed my sheep" (**John 21:15-17**).
- **David** fell into sin with Bathsheba, but after repentance, God still used him and kept His promise through David's line (**2 Samuel 12-13, Psalm 51**).
- **Paul** was literally persecuting Christians, but God flipped his whole life and made him one of the greatest apostles (**Acts 9**).

So here's the real leadership lesson, leaders fail, but leaders also get back up. **Proverbs 24:16** says, "The righteous falls seven times and rises again." You're not defined by the smash, you're defined by whether you go back up the mountain and let God rewrite your story.

If you're sitting in a cell right now, maybe you smashed your life and feel like it's over. If you're running a business and you tanked it, maybe you feel like there's no recovery. If you're a father or husband who blew it at home, maybe you think you can't earn back trust. I'm telling you, there's hope after failure. God is in the business of fresh starts.

So here's the question, will you stay stuck staring at the broken pieces, or will you pick up some new tablets and climb back up to God?

Handle That

Write down one area of your life where you've smashed what God gave you. Business, family, ministry, reputation. Then write how God might be calling you back to start fresh. What would it look like to "cut some new tablets" and let Him rewrite your story?

Take Note

- Where have I failed as a leader, and how can I let God redeem that?
- Who in my life needs me to show them that second chances are real?
- What mountain do I need to climb back up instead of staying in shame?
- Am I willing to accept a fresh start, or am I holding myself hostage to my past?

Take It to God

Father, thank You for being the God of second chances. I've broken things You trusted me with, and I've failed more times than I can count, but You still call me back up the mountain. Help me not stay stuck in shame. Teach me to accept Your renewal, and to lead others with grace because I've received grace. Rewrite the broken places in my life and turn them into testimonies. **In Jesus' Name, Amen.**

The Power of Second Chances

Moses was supposed to be God's leader, but early on this dude caught a body and ran. Instead of leading Israel, he ended up hiding in Midian, tending sheep, thinking his shot was over. That should have been the end of the story, but God pulled him back in (Michael Corleone voice). He got another shot at leadership. Another chance to do right.

And check this, the same Moses who thought he was disqualified became the one God used to split seas, call down plagues, and deliver His people. That's the power of second chances.

So let me ask you, who deserves second chances? Do you? Do the people who betrayed you? The folks that messed up in your family? The homie that relapsed again? The employee that failed? The truth is, God specializes in giving second chances, but as leaders we struggle to give them.

Why do we count people out so quickly? Why do we think our failure disqualifies us forever? Leaders who understand God's mercy know how to extend mercy. Leaders who've been given grace should be quick to give grace.

Now, don't get it twisted, second chances don't mean no consequences. Moses still had to flee Egypt. David still faced fallout in his family. But God doesn't waste broken people. He rebuilds them. And He uses them to lead with more humility and empathy than before.

Think about your life. Are you writing yourself off because of your past? Are you saying, "Nah, God can't use me, I messed up too bad"? Or are you the leader holding grudges, refusing to give someone else another shot? Both are dangerous. Both miss the heart of God.

Jesus told Peter to forgive "seventy times seven" (**Matthew 18:22**). Not because people deserve it, but because forgiveness frees you. Leaders who can't forgive end up bitter, and bitter leaders can't lead.

So what's your move? Are you willing to receive the second chance God's offering you? And are you willing to extend second chances to others, even when it's hard?

Handle That

Think of one area in your life where you need to receive God's second chance. Write it down. Then think of one person you've been refusing to forgive or give another shot. Pray about it. Maybe it's time to let them breathe again, just like God did with you.

Take Note

- Where have I disqualified myself when God has already forgiven me?
- Who in my life needs me to extend a second chance?
- How do I balance grace with accountability as a leader?
- Do I lead with a heart that reflects God's mercy, or with a heart that stays stuck in bitterness?

Take It to God

Father, thank You for being the God of second chances. Thank You for not giving up on me when I messed up. Help me to forgive and extend mercy like You do. Remind me that failure is not the end of the story, and that You can still use me and those around me for Your glory. Teach me to lead with grace, because I've been given grace. **In Jesus' Name, Amen.**

When the Messenger Got a Record

"After looking in all directions to make sure no one was watching, Moses killed the Egyptian and hid the body in the sand." - (Exodus 2:12 NLT)

Life and Leadership Lesson

Before Moses ever held the Ten Commandments that said **"You shall not murder,"** he had already caught a body. That's wild when you think about it. The very messenger of God, the one chosen to deliver the law and split seas, had a record that should've disqualified him. And yet, God still used him. Imagine that, the one God would use to deliver His people, starting off with blood on his hands.

Have you ever felt guilty because you're telling people not to do the same thing you once did? Maybe you're preaching sobriety but you once drowned in addiction. Maybe you're mentoring kids to stay off the block but you once ran the streets yourself. Maybe you're building a business with integrity but you used to scam to survive. Maybe you're telling folks to walk holy while you know your own past is full of dirt.

Maybe you've been in the system, done time, or maybe your record is addiction, broken marriages, cheating, anger, lying, or betrayal. That voice in your head starts whispering, "Who do you think you are? You ain't qualified. You're a hypocrite." And if you're not careful, that guilt will paralyze you.

Moses had a record. David had one too, remember? He set up Uriah to die after committing adultery with Bathsheba (**2 Samuel 11**). Paul had a record, he was out here persecuting and killing Christians before he became an apostle (**Acts 8:1-3, Acts 9:1**). Peter had a record of denial (**Luke 22:54-62**), he denied Jesus three times. Yet these are the very people God used to flip the world upside down.

Here's the lesson: your past disqualifies you in man's eyes, but it positions you in God's. Your scars become your sermon. Your failures become your testimony. That's what makes your leadership hit harder, you're not preaching theory, you're speaking from experience.

Now let's get personal. Are you letting your record hold you back? Are you hiding in shame like Moses burying that Egyptian in the sand, hoping nobody digs it up? Or are you bold enough to let God redeem your story and use it as fuel to lead others?

The truth is, people don't need perfect leaders, they need real ones. Real recognizes real. They need to see someone who's been through the fire and still stands. They need to see that the God who forgave you can forgive them too.

Leadership ain't about pretending you've never fallen. It's about admitting you fell and showing others how to get back up. Paul said it best in **1 Timothy 1:15-16**, ***"Christ Jesus came into the world to save sinners, of whom I am the foremost. But I received mercy for this reason, that in me... Jesus Christ might display his perfect patience as an example to those who were to believe in him."***

Crazy, right? Paul was basically saying, "If God can use me, He can use anyone."

So I'll ask you: are you still disqualifying yourself because of your past? Are you letting shame keep you quiet when your story could set someone else free? Are you letting the record define you, or are you letting God rewrite it?

You see where I'm going? God doesn't pick perfect people. He picks willing ones. That's why this chapter is for you, especially for those of us who came out of dark places. The very thing you think disqualifies you may be the thing that makes you relatable to the people God is sending you to. Moses knew what it was like to fail. That gave him compassion when leading people who failed over and over in the desert.

So here's the real lesson.. Don't hide from your record, but don't stay stuck in it either. Moses ran away after this moment. He thought his purpose was done. But God wasn't done with him. What about you? Have you buried something in the sand and think that's it? Are you convinced God can't use you because of your past? Or are you willing to let Him rewrite your story?

Listen, leadership isn't about being perfect, just be faithful. That means when your past screams at you, you remind yourself what Paul said in **2 Corinthians 5:17**: *"This means that anyone who belongs to Christ has become a new person. The old life is gone; a new life has begun!"* That's crazy, but it's real.

So, whether you're an inmate reading this in your cell or a business owner dealing with shame behind closed doors, this is for you to remember, your record does not disqualify you, it might just be the reason people will listen to you.

Handle That

Write down one part of your past that still makes you feel unworthy. Then flip it, ask yourself, "How can God use this exact thing as part of my message to others?" Don't hide it in the sand. Put it in God's hands.

Take Note

- What guilt or shame from my past is still holding me back from serving and leading boldly?
- Do I see myself as disqualified, or as redeemed and called?
- Who in my life needs to hear my story so they know God can use them too?
- Am I letting my scars stay hidden, or am I letting them testify?
- What am I still hiding in the sand, afraid for people to know?
- How could my story of failure actually serve as a bridge for others?

Take It to God

Father, thank You that my past does not define me. Just like You didn't throw Moses away when he messed up, You haven't thrown me away either. Teach me how to walk in forgiveness and freedom. Show me how to turn my record into a testimony that lifts others up. Help me not to hide from my failures but to let You redeem them for Your glory. Thank You for using broken people with records and scars to lead Your people. Forgive me for letting guilt and shame silence me. Remind me that my past is not my prison, it's my platform. Teach me to lead with humility, honesty, and boldness. Help me to use my scars to point others to Your healing. **In Jesus' Name, Amen.**

Chapter 32

Rejection Ain't the End of the Story

"Moses returned to the Lord and said, 'Why, Lord, why have you brought trouble on this people? Is this why you sent me? Ever since I went to Pharaoh to speak in your name, he has brought trouble on this people, and you have not rescued your people at all." - (Exodus 5:22-23)

"Then the Lord said to Moses, 'Now you will see what I will do to Pharaoh: Because of my mighty hand he will let them go; because of my mighty hand he will drive them out of his country." - (Exodus 6:1)

(Isaiah 41:9-10, Psalm 118:22, Romans 8:31)

Life and Leadership Lesson

Crazy. Moses obeyed God, went to Pharaoh, and instead of seeing breakthrough, he got slammed with rejection. Not only did Pharaoh clown him, but the people he was trying to help turned against him too. Imagine the weight, you're doing what God told you, and it looks like everything backfired. That's a leader's nightmare.

Rejection hurts because it attacks your identity. It makes you question your call. "Why did You send me, God? Did I hear You wrong? Am I even built for this?" Moses felt it. You've felt it. I've felt it.

When Moses approached Pharoah 10 times, not once or twice, 10 times! When was the last time you were rejected like that?

But here's the thing, rejection does not mean disqualification. It just means redirection. God had to remind Moses, "Chill. I'm still in control. You're about to see what I will do." That's the reminder for every leader, entrepreneur, pastor, or inmate, rejection is not the end of the story, it's often the setup for God to flex His power.

Think about it:

- **Joseph** was rejected by his own brothers, sold into slavery, and thrown into prison, but God used that rejection to position him to save a nation (**Genesis 50:20**).
- **David** was rejected by Saul, hunted like a dog, but that rejection pushed him into the wilderness where God shaped him into a king (**1 Samuel 22**).
- **Jesus** Himself was *"despised and rejected by men"* (Isaiah 53:3). He was rejected in His own hometown (**Mark 6:4**). Even His disciples dipped out on Him when it got tough. But through that rejection came the cross, and through the cross came salvation for the world.

Boom. If Jesus Himself faced rejection, why do we think we won't?

So, who's rejected you? Was it your family, your friends, your old crew, your boss, maybe even your own church? How did it shape you? Did it make you bitter, or did it push you closer to God?

Rejection trauma is real. Some of us carry wounds from parents who never affirmed us, relationships that broke us, business deals that went south, or communities that turned their back. Leaders, don't front, you can be on top in public and still feel unwanted in private.

Here's the truth: rejection is painful, but it's also a tool in God's hands. It can strip away pride, deepen your dependence on Him, and position you exactly where He needs you. **Psalm 118:22** says, ***"The stone that the builders rejected has become the cornerstone."*** What people throw away, God builds with.

So here's the question, are you letting rejection define you, or are you letting God refine you through it?

Handle That

Write down one rejection that still haunts you. Take it to God in prayer this week. Then flip it, write one way that rejection shaped you for the better. How can you use that story to lead others who feel unwanted?

Take Note

- Where in my life has rejection left scars?
- Have I let rejection make me bitter, or has it pushed me toward God?
- How do I respond when people I lead reject me?
- Do I believe that God can turn rejection into redirection?

Take It to God

Father, You know the sting of rejection. You know the pain it brings and the doubts it plants. Help me not to see rejection as the end of my story but as part of Your plan to shape me. Heal the wounds that rejection has left in my heart. Teach me to lead with compassion, even when I've been hurt. Remind me that if Jesus was rejected, I shouldn't be surprised when I am too. Give me strength to keep moving forward. **In Jesus' Name, Amen.**

Chapter 33

The Encourager

"And Moses said to the people, Fear not, stand firm, and see the salvation of the Lord, which he will work for you today. For the Egyptians whom you see today, you shall never see again. The Lord will fight for you, and you have only to be silent." - (Exodus 14:13-14 ESV)

"But I said to you, Don't be shocked or afraid of them! The Lord your God is going ahead of you. He will fight for you, just as you saw him do in Egypt. And you saw how the Lord your God cared for you all along the way as you traveled through the wilderness, just as a father cares for his child. Now he has brought you to this place." - (Deuteronomy 1:29-31 NLT)

"Be strong and courageous. Do not fear or be in dread of them, for it is the Lord your God who goes with you. He will not leave you or forsake you. … It is the Lord who goes before you. He will be with you; he will not leave you or forsake you. Do not fear or be dismayed." - (Deuteronomy 31:6,8 ESV)

Life and Leadership Lesson

Moses didn't just drop commands, he dropped encouragement. He told the people not to trip, not to panic, because God was already going before them. He reminded them of what God already did in Egypt. He reminded them of how God carried them like a father carries his kid. That's encouragement at its highest level, pointing people back to God's faithfulness.

Moses was constantly encouraging people. When they hit the Red Sea (**Exodus 14**), he told them, *"Don't be afraid, watch the Lord fight for you."* When they were freaking out about food, he reminded them that God would provide manna (**Exodus 16**). When they were worried about water, he encouraged them with God's promise to bring it out of a rock (**Exodus 17:6**).

When Joshua was about to step into leadership, Moses encouraged him directly: *"Be strong and courageous. Do not be afraid or terrified because of them, for the Lord your God goes with you" (Deuteronomy 31:6-8).* Think about it. When Joshua took over, God told him three times, *"Be strong and courageous" (Joshua 1:6-9)*. Why? Because encouragement fuels courage.

But Moses ain't the only one. Look at Jonathan with David in **1 Samuel 23:16**, he went to David in the wilderness and **"helped him find strength in God."** Boom. That's what a real encourager does, they don't just hype you up with motivational quotes, they point you back to God's strength.

Look at Barnabas in **Acts 11:23**, when he arrived and saw what the grace of God had done, *"he was glad and encouraged them all to remain true to the Lord with all their hearts."* His whole name meant *son of encouragement.* He encouraged Paul when nobody else wanted to touch him because of his past (**Acts 9:27**). That one word of encouragement opened the door for Paul's entire ministry. That's wild. Paul told the Thessalonians, *"Encourage one another and build one another up" (1 Thessalonians 5:11).*

Even Jesus was an encourager. He told His disciples in **John 16:33**, *"Take heart, because I have overcome the world."* He encouraged Peter after his denial by restoring him in **John 21**, telling him to feed His sheep. Jesus didn't cancel Peter, He encouraged him to keep moving in his calling.

So let me ask you:

- Who are you encouraging right now?
- When was the last time you looked somebody in the eye and said, "You got this, God is with you"?
- Do people feel stronger in their faith after being around you, or more drained?
- As a leader, whether you're running a crew, a business, or a family, are you known for criticizing or for encouraging?

Encouragement ain't soft. It keeps people from quitting. It gives people hope in hopeless situations. It strengthens hearts for the fight. Leaders who don't encourage won't have followers for long, because nobody wants to run with someone who only points out what's wrong.

Here's the thing, every leader needs to know how to encourage. Sometimes people don't need another lecture, they need life spoken into them. My wife does that for me all the time. I remember the day before my very for men's retreat that I was organizing, I had gotten into it with a family member and the whole situation really discouraged me. I didn't have it in me to go up a mountain and speak to men about being strong in the middle of me being weak. My wife was like *"Oh no you're not, you're not gonna sit here and be outright disobedient because of an argument! God put this retreat on your heart and He gave you this assignment for these men. You get up, and remember everything that God is doing for us right now, you're not gonna be disobedient now. You go to this retreat, and encourage these men, and if you don't have it in you then you go and be encouraged by the men God sent there!"*

So let me ask you: when's the last time you encouraged your people? When's the last time you looked at your team, your family, your church, or even your cellmate and said, "Fear not, God's got this"? Do you speak life, or do you drain it?

Leaders don't just give orders, they give hope. They remind the people what God has already done, like Moses saying, ***"Remember Egypt, remember the wilderness, remember how God carried us."*** They point people back to God's track record.

Now, flip it, Who has encouraged you when you wanted to give up? Maybe it was a parent, a mentor, a pastor, a homie who saw something in you when you couldn't see it in yourself. What did their words do for you? Leaders need to pay that forward.

Encouragement doesn't mean faking it or sugarcoating. It means speaking truth with faith. Moses wasn't blind, he saw the Red Sea and Pharaoh's army. But he also saw God's faithfulness. He shifted the people's focus from fear to faith. That's what true encouragers do.

Anybody can tear people down. Real leaders build people up. Real leaders put courage back into the discouraged.

Handle That

Ask yourself, Who encouraged me into my calling? How can I do that for someone else? Think of three people in your circle who are discouraged right now. Write down one specific way you can encourage each of them. Call them, text them, pull them aside, whatever, but speak life into them. Don't wait. Be the reason someone didn't give up on their passion, goal, dream, calling.

Take Note

- What encouragement from others has kept me from giving up?
- Do I build up my kids, team, or friends, or do I mainly correct and criticize?
- Who has God placed in my life right now that needs encouragement to keep going?
- Am I speaking life to the people I lead, or am I just pointing out their flaws?
- Do I remind people of God's past faithfulness when they're scared about the future?
- Do I leave people more fearful or more faithful after talking to me?

Take It to God

Father, thank You for placing encouragers in my life who reminded me of Your power when I wanted to give up. Teach me to be that kind of leader, one who speaks life, one who builds up and not tears down. Give me words that put courage back into discouraged hearts. Help me to shift people's focus from fear to faith. Help me to remind others of Your faithfulness and point them back to Your strength. Use my words to lift people up, whether they're in a cell, in a business, in a pulpit, or at a kitchen table. Make me bold enough to speak life when others want to give up. **In Jesus' Name, Amen**

Chapter 34

When the Pillars Disappear, Trust Him

"By day the Lord went ahead of them in a pillar of cloud to guide them on their way and by night in a pillar of fire to give them light, so that they could travel by day or night. Neither the pillar of cloud by day nor the pillar of fire by night left its place in front of the people." - (Exodus 13:21-22)

Life and Leadership Lesson

I mean what other proof do you need that says "I got you!" Every day they looked up and saw a cloud leading them. Every night they looked up and saw fire lighting the way. They didn't need GPS, Google Maps, or a five-year business plan. They just had to follow the pillar. For real though, would you ever doubt God after those signs and miracles? We would like to believe no one would ever doubt how real he is after that, but these guys forgot real quick!

But let's be real. What happens when the pillar disappears? What happens when you don't feel God's presence, when the signs aren't clear, when the path looks dark? Most leaders panic right there. They think if they don't see the pillar, God must've bounced. But the truth is, God's presence was never gone. The pillar was just the visible reminder.

Have you ever been in that season where you couldn't feel God at all? Maybe you're sitting in a cell right now, and it feels like your prayers are hitting the ceiling. Maybe you're a business owner staring at empty accounts wondering where God is. Maybe you're a pastor who feels like you've lost the fire. That's what it feels like when the pillars disappear.

But here's the thing, faith isn't built on feelings, it's built on trust. **Hebrews 11:1** says, ***"Now faith is confidence in what we hope for and assurance about what we do not see."*** Boom. That means sometimes you gotta walk even when you don't see the fire in the sky.

David felt this too. In **Psalm 13** he said, ***"How long, Lord? Will you forget me forever? How long will you hide your face from me?"*** That's a man after God's heart, feeling abandoned. But by the end of the psalm he says, *"But I trust in your unfailing love."* The pillars may disappear, but God doesn't.

As leaders, we need to understand this. Whether you're leading a church, a company, a crew on the block, or just your family. you can't depend on feelings to guide you. Feelings will lie. Signs will fade. But God's Word never changes. **Proverbs 3:5–6 says, *"Trust in the Lord with all your heart and lean not on your own understanding; in all your ways submit to him, and he will make your paths straight."***

So let me ask you: what do you do when you don't see the pillar? Do you quit? Do you freeze up? Or do you keep trusting that God is still leading, even when you don't see the proof?

Real leaders keep moving by faith, not sight. Paul said it in **2 Corinthians 5:7,** *"For we walk by faith, not by sight."* That's the difference between leaders who last and leaders who crumble.

Handle That

Identify one area in your life right now where it feels like the pillar has disappeared. Write it down. Instead of waiting for a sign, decide to trust God in that area and take one step forward by faith this week.

Take Note

- Where in my life does it feel like the pillar is gone?
- Am I waiting on feelings instead of trusting God's Word?
- What step of faith do I need to take even when I don't "see" the way?

Take It to God

Father, I admit sometimes I panic when I don't see the signs or feel Your presence. Forgive me for doubting You when the pillars seem to disappear. Teach me to trust You by faith and not by sight. Help me as a leader to walk steady, even when I don't feel steady. Remind me that You never left, and You never will. Strengthen my trust in You today. **In Jesus' Name, Amen.**

Chapter 35

Leading With Humility

"Now Moses was very humble, more humble than any other person on earth."
- (Numbers 12:3 NLT)

Life and Leadership Lesson

Let's be real, leadership comes with weight. When you're in charge, people look to you for answers, direction, vision, and even how to react under pressure. That spotlight can make your head big real quick. You start believing your own hype. You start thinking the success is because of you, your smarts, your grind, your voice. That's when leaders fall.

But Moses? The Bible says this dude was the meekest man alive. Think about that. He had just led millions of people out of slavery, walked them through the Red Sea, brought down plagues on Egypt, and yet God still called him humble. That's crazy. Most of us would've been walking around like, "Yeah, I did that." But Moses knew, it wasn't him. It was God working through him.

Here's the kicker though. That line about Moses' humility shows up in *Numbers 12*, right after his own brother Aaron and sister Miriam start talking trash about him. They're like, ***"Who does Moses think he is? God speaks through us too."*** Imagine your own family questioning your call. Most of us would've clapped back, flexed credentials, reminded them who parted the Red Sea. But Moses? He stayed silent and let God handle it. God Himself came down in the cloud and defended Moses.

That's leadership. That's humility. Letting God fight your battles instead of trying to prove yourself.

And that same principle runs through the whole Bible. ***Proverbs 22:4*** says, ***"The reward for humility and fear of the Lord is riches and honor and life."*** *James 4:10* says, ***"Humble yourselves before the Lord, and He will exalt you."*** Jesus Himself said in ***Matthew 23:11, "The greatest among you shall be your servant."***

So let me ask you, are you leading with humility, or are you leading with ego? Do you walk into the room needing everybody to recognize your position, your title, your hustle? Or do you walk in ready to serve, ready to listen, ready to learn?

Look at Jesus. The Son of God, Creator of everything, washed His disciples' feet (**John 13:12-15**). He could've called angels to serve Him, but instead He grabbed a towel and got down on the floor. That's humility in action. That's the model of leadership.

Paul backs it up in **Philippians 2:3-4**, *"Do nothing from selfish ambition or conceit, but in humility count others more significant than yourselves. Let each of you look not only to his own interests, but also to the interests of others."* That's not just pretty words, that's the grind of leadership.

Maybe you're running a business, maybe you're leading a crew, maybe you're in prison trying to guide younger dudes on the yard, the question stays the same: Are you leading with humility or control? Do people follow you because they respect you, or because they fear you?

Humility doesn't mean weakness. It doesn't mean being a doormat. It means knowing your strength comes from God and pointing people back to Him instead of yourself. Moses had authority, but he didn't abuse it. He carried the weight with a bowed heart.

So let's bring it to you: If God lifted you up in this season, are you humble enough to not take the credit? If your name blew up, if your brand started trending, if your ministry doubled, would you still give God the glory? Or would you start believing it was all you?

Handle That

- Write down the areas where pride creeps in. Be real with yourself.
- Start practicing humility by serving in secret. Do something nobody else knows about and don't post it, don't brag about it.
- Remember, leadership isn't about the spotlight. It's about stewardship.

Take Note

- Do I lead with humility, or am I chasing recognition?
- How do I react when people question me or misunderstand me? Do I defend myself, or let God do it?
- Am I serving the people I lead, or am I expecting them to serve me?

Take It to God

Father, teach me to lead with humility like Moses and like Jesus. Strip away pride, ego, and the need to be recognized. Help me to serve others first, to count their needs before my own. And when people misunderstand me or even come against me, give me the wisdom to stay quiet and let You fight my battles. Make me into the kind of leader who points people back to You instead of myself. **In Jesus Name, Amen.**

The Traits of a Leader

"Moreover, look for able men from all the people, men who fear God, who are trustworthy and hate a bribe, and place such men over the people as chiefs of thousands, of hundreds, of fifties, and of tens. And let them judge the people at all times. Every great matter they shall bring to you, but any small matter they shall decide themselves. So it will be easier for you, and they will bear the burden with you." - (Exodus 18:21-22 ESV)

"Then the Lord said to Moses, 'Gather for me seventy men of the elders of Israel, whom you know to be the elders of the people and officers over them, and bring them to the tent of meeting, and let them take their stand there with you. And I will come down and talk with you there. And I will take some of the Spirit that is on you and put it on them, and they shall bear the burden of the people with you, so that you may not bear it yourself alone.'" - (Numbers 11:16-17 ESV)

Life and Leadership Lesson

Crazy right? God didn't say, "Go grab seventy random dudes." He told Moses to pick *elders he knew*. People already proven, respected, tested. Leadership ain't a popularity contest. It's about character, wisdom, and the Spirit of God resting on you. Here's the deal, Moses was exhausted. He was sitting from morning to night listening to every stinkin' problem, every dispute, every little thing that came up. Imagine a whole nation lined up at your door saying, "He said this, she did that, I need this fixed." That's not leadership, that's suicide by stress. And Jethro saw it. He loved Moses enough to say, ***"Son, what you're doing isn't good. You're gonna wear yourself out, and the people too."***

Let's go back. Jethro, Moses' father-in-law, already gave him the blueprint in **Exodus 18:21**. He told him to pick ***"able men from all the people, men who fear God, who are trustworthy and hate a bribe."*** Boom. That's the checklist, that's how you build a team.

But notice Jethro didn't just say, "Go get help." He gave a **blueprint**. He listed traits. Because not everybody deserves a seat at the table. Not everybody is cut out for leadership. Here's the four traits he laid out:

1. **Able men** - Capable, skilled, not just talkers but doers. People who can actually handle responsibility without folding under pressure.
2. **Fear God** - Not just talented but submitted. They care more about God's approval than man's applause.
3. **Trustworthy** - People of integrity. What they say in public matches what they do in private.
4. **Hate a bribe** - You can't buy them. They don't fold when money, influence, or pressure comes.

Think about that. How different would our churches, businesses, and communities look if we picked leaders with these traits? How different would your circle look if you applied this filter before giving somebody trust?

But how many of us surround ourselves with the wrong people? With yes-men, hype men, or shady characters who look loyal but ain't got the Spirit of God in them? That's wild. If you're building a business, who's on your team? If you're leading your family, who's speaking into your kids' lives? If you're doing time, who's sitting at your table in the yard?

The Bible's loaded with traits of real leaders. Paul told Timothy the kind of people to put in leadership: ***"Above reproach, sober-minded, self-controlled, respectable, hospitable, able to teach" (1 Timothy 3:2)***. He told Titus the same, **leaders shouldn't be arrogant, quick-tempered, drunkards, violent, or greedy (Titus 1:7-9)**. That ain't just for pastors. That's for anyone leading others.

David's mighty men are another example **(2 Samuel 23)**. They risked their lives to bring David water from Bethlehem even when he didn't ask. These weren't just tough dudes, they were loyal to the mission. One fought a lion in a pit on a snowy day. Another killed 800 with a spear. But beyond the action, they carried loyalty and courage that matched David's heart.

Nehemiah had the same thing. When he rebuilt Jerusalem's wall **(Nehemiah 3)**, he had families, priests, and workers shoulder to shoulder. They weren't rich, they weren't fancy, but they were committed. They built while holding swords. That's the kind of crew you need, ready to build and fight at the same time.

That's the type of soldiers you want in your circle. Not dudes who dip when things get hard, but ones who move with you even through the fire.

And here's something personal, what traits do *you* carry? Are you the kind of person someone else would trust to lead? Or do you need God to strip some junk out of you first? This ain't just about who's on your team. It's about you being worthy of someone else's team.

Let me ask you, do the people around you fear God or fear missing out? Do they hate corruption or secretly chase it? Are they trustworthy with little, or do they crack under pressure? Are you picking leaders based on hype, looks, or skill, but ignoring character?

Take inventory of your circle. Write down the names of three people you trust to help you carry the weight. Then check them against the traits Jethro laid out: fear God, trustworthy, hate bribes. If they don't measure up, maybe you need to pray for God to send some Aarons, Hurs, and elders into your life.

That's the reality for a lot of us. Leaders in business, pastors in ministry, even a shot caller on the block, we think we gotta hold it all together by ourselves. But the truth is, if you don't learn to delegate, you're gonna burn out and crash.

Jesus lived this principle too. He didn't just randomly pick disciples. He prayed all night before choosing the twelve (**Luke 6:12-13**). He wasn't looking for perfect men, but He was looking for ones willing to be shaped, corrected, and stretched.

Paul told Timothy the same blueprint. **2 Timothy 2:2** says, **"Now teach these truths to other trustworthy people who will be able to pass them on to others."** That's leadership DNA. You're not just teaching for now, you're building something that outlives you.

Here's a question for you: Who's on your team right now? Are they trustworthy? Do they fear God? Or are you giving influence to someone who can be bought with a quick payday or a pat on the back?

Let's be real, a lot of us get in trouble because we hand leadership or influence to the wrong people. Maybe it's that flashy friend who talks smooth but don't fear God. Maybe it's that cousin you trust because he's family, but his character ain't matching up. Maybe it's a business partner who loves money more than the mission. And when it falls apart, you sit back like, "Man, how did I not see that coming?"

Jethro gave us the answer, check the traits. Don't just look at the hustle, look at the heart. Don't just look at ability, look at integrity. Because talent without character is dangerous. Leadership without character will collapse. That's true in business, ministry, politics, even the streets. We've all seen it. You put the wrong people in charge, and the whole crew goes down.

So I'll ask you straight up: Who are you letting speak into your life? Who are you putting in leadership positions around you? Who's holding you accountable? And are you yourself walking in those traits, or are you expecting others to carry what you won't?

Handle That

Don't just build a team, build the right team. And remember, sometimes subtraction is addition, losing the wrong person is making room for the right one. Today, take the time to restructure your circle by Jethro's traits.

Take Note

- Take a hard look at your inner circle. Do they fear God? Are they trustworthy? Or are you keeping people around out of comfort or history?
- If you're in leadership, write out the traits you look for before you give anyone a role or responsibility. Compare that with Jethro's list.
- Am I surrounding myself with yes-men or truth-tellers?
- Do I lead with character, or just charisma?
- Would God choose me if He was picking 70 today?
- Do I fear God more than I fear man?
- Am I trustworthy with what God has already given me?
- Do I have the courage to hate compromise and stay clean, even when it costs me?
- Who am I raising up that can carry the load with me?

Take It to God

Father, thank You for showing me through Moses and Jethro what real leadership looks like. Teach me to recognize the traits that matter: honesty, integrity, the fear of God. Give me discernment to know who belongs in my circle and who doesn't. Protect me from trusting the wrong voices. Make me into the kind of leader who carries these traits so I can multiply them into others. And help me never forget that leadership isn't about power, it's about service. Forgive me for the times I've trusted the wrong people or overlooked character for convenience. Teach me to build my team with people who fear You, who walk with integrity, and who carry Your Spirit.

And make me into that kind of leader too, trustworthy, faithful, steady, and real. Don't just let me pick the right people, make me the right person. **In Jesus' Name, Amen.**

Make Them Stop

"Joshua son of Nun, who had been Moses' aide since youth, spoke up and said, 'Moses, my lord, stop them!' But Moses replied, 'Are you jealous for my sake? I wish that all the Lord's people were prophets and that the Lord would put his Spirit on them!'" - (Exodus 18:21-23)

Life and Leadership Lesson

Here's the scene. God poured out His Spirit on seventy elders, and they started prophesying. But two of them, Eldad and Medad, weren't even at the tent. They were out in the camp, but the Spirit hit them too. Word spread, and Joshua, Moses' right-hand man, got jealous. He runs up to Moses and says, *"Make them stop!"*

Now pause. Joshua wasn't being shady, he thought he was protecting Moses. He didn't want anyone stealing his leader's shine. But Moses? Moses hit him with wisdom: *"Are you jealous for my sake? I wish all God's people had the Spirit."*

Boom. That's wild. Moses didn't see other leaders as a threat. He saw them as reinforcements. He knew leadership was never about clout, it was about the Spirit of God.

So let me ask you, how do you handle it when people around you misunderstand what God is doing? Have you ever had someone in your corner get jealous for you, when you weren't even jealous for yourself? Or maybe you've been Joshua, looking sideways at someone else's gift because it wasn't what you were used to.

Jealousy will creep in when you don't understand that God's Spirit isn't limited. Leaders who are insecure see others as competition. Leaders who are mature see others as co-laborers. Moses wasn't worried about losing power, because he knew his assignment was from God.

Joshua had to learn that real leadership isn't about protecting the spotlight, it's about multiplying the mission. That's why later, when Joshua finally became the leader, he carried that same Spirit forward. He learned from Moses not to be threatened by God raising up others, but to embrace it.

And that's the challenge for us. In business, in ministry, even on the streets, are you secure enough to celebrate someone else's success? Or do you feel threatened when others rise up? Do you try to make them stop, or do you recognize God's hand on them?

Yo, hear me out, if you're jealous of someone else's gift, you've forgotten where your own gift came from. The Spirit don't run out. God pouring into someone else doesn't mean He's taking away from you.

Handle That

Think about someone you've been jealous of, maybe it's their influence, their business, their platform, their gift. Instead of asking God to make them stop, pray for them and ask God to bless their work. Then ask God to show you how your lane and their lane can work together.

Take Note

- Have you ever been Joshua, jealous for someone's sake or even jealous yourself?
- Are you mature enough to celebrate when God's Spirit moves through others?
- What would happen in your leadership if you saw other leaders as allies, not competition?

Take It to God

Father, forgive me for the times I've been jealous, insecure, or threatened by others. Teach me to see Your Spirit at work in people around me and to celebrate it, not fight it. Give me a heart like Moses, a leader who wanted everyone filled with Your Spirit. Help me handle misunderstandings with wisdom and security, and let me build others up instead of tearing them down. **In Jesus' Name, Amen.**

Chapter 36

No Credit Needed

"Then the Lord said to Moses, 'Gather for me seventy men of the elders of Israel, whom you know to be the elders of the people and officers over them, and bring them to the tent of meeting, and let them take their stand there with you. And I will come down and talk with you there. And I will take some of the Spirit that is on you and put it on them, and they shall bear the burden of the people with you, so that you may not bear it yourself alone." - (Numbers 11:16-17 ESV)

"...so that your giving may be in secret. And your Father who sees in secret will reward you." - (Matthew 6:4 ESV)

Life and Leadership Lesson

Let's get real, everybody wants their flowers, their applause, their name in lights. But leadership in the Kingdom of God ain't about credit, it's about carrying the weight faithfully. When God told Moses to pick seventy elders, He didn't give us all their names. You can't rattle them off like you do Moses, Joshua, or David. But those men carried the burden of a nation. They mattered, even if history never put their names on a billboard.

Think about that. God chose them, gave them His Spirit, and they served faithfully. And yet they stayed in the shadows. That's leadership at its purest, being faithful when nobody sees you.

And this ain't just them. The Bible is full of faceless, nameless heroes:

- **The little boy** who handed over his five loaves and two fish in **John 6**. We don't know his name, but millions of people read his story. Thousands were fed because he gave what he had. No credit, just obedience.
- **The four friends** who carried the paralyzed man to Jesus in **Mark 2**. We don't know their names, but without them, their homie never makes it to the roof and into healing. Their faith literally carried him to his miracle.
- **The widow** in **Mark 12** who gave two small coins. We don't know her name, but Jesus said she gave more than anybody else. No clout, no fame, just faith.
- **The man who gave Jesus his donkey** for the triumphal entry **(Luke 19)**. We don't know who he was, but his small act fulfilled prophecy and set the stage for Palm Sunday.

These are nobodies on paper, but heroes in God's eyes.

Let me ask you, are you willing to be that kind of leader? Are you okay being the one who makes the play but doesn't get their name in the box score? Would you still show up if nobody clapped, if nobody followed you on Instagram, if nobody remembered your name?

Moses needed those seventy elders. Jesus needed that boy's bread. Paul needed Ananias, the man who prayed for him when he was blind **(Acts 9)**. Ananias ain't famous, but his obedience launched Paul's ministry.

Here's the raw truth: most of the Kingdom runs on nameless servants. You might be a mom raising kids in secret, a brother leading Bible study in a prison cell, or a businessman funding ministries without your name on a plaque. Heaven sees it all.

Real leaders don't chase credit. They chase obedience. They know **Matthew 6** is true, God Himself will reward what's done in secret. That reward hits different, because it's eternal.

Handle That

- Do something this week for someone that nobody will ever know you did.
- Ask yourself: If I never get credit, am I still down to serve?
- Pray for a heart that values obedience over applause.

Take Note

- Who are the "nameless" leaders in my life who impacted me?
- Am I willing to lead in secret, without being noticed?
- What's one area where I've been chasing recognition instead of faithfulness?

Take It to God

Father, thank You for the nameless and faceless heroes who carried Your work forward without seeking glory. Teach me to be faithful in the shadows. Strip away my need for recognition, and help me to remember that You see every sacrifice, every prayer, every act of service. Make me a leader who serves because of love, not applause. And remind me that Your reward is greater than anything this world can offer. **In Jesus' Name, Amen.**

It's Ok to Be Second

"Thus the Lord used to speak to Moses face to face, as a man speaks to his friend. When Moses turned again into the camp, his assistant Joshua the son of Nun, a young man, would not depart from the tent." - (Exodus 33:11 ESV)

Life and Leadership Lesson

Think about that picture for a second. Moses, the man of God, goes into the tent, talks with God like a friend, then leaves. Everybody knows Moses is the guy in charge, the one with the staff, the one splitting seas, the one climbing mountains. But look at Joshua, the young buck, the assistant. He's not in the spotlight, he's not writing laws, he's not the one everyone's following. But what does he do? He lingers. He hangs out. He stays in the presence of God long after Moses leaves.

That's heavy. Because real leadership starts in the shadows, not the spotlight. Joshua was willing to sit in second place so he could learn what first place feels like. He wasn't salty that Moses had the shine. He wasn't itching to grab the mic. He was just faithful to be near God.

Ask yourself, are you good with being number two? Or do you always have to be the top dog? Do you always need your name on the flyer, or can you faithfully serve somebody else's dream and let God elevate you in His timing? Where's your heart at?

Most people want the crown but not the cross. Joshua teaches us patience. He teaches us that second place ain't failure, it's prep work. You can't be trusted to lead if you don't know how to serve.

Look at David. Before he was king, he was just a kid running errands, bringing bread and cheese to his brothers (**1 Samuel 17:17-18**). Imagine if David had said, "Nah, send someone else." He would've missed his shot at Goliath. Serving put him in the right place at the right time.

Look at Elisha. Before he was a prophet, he was just following Elijah, washing his hands, carrying his cloak. No shine, no platform, just faithful. Then God hit him with a double portion (**2 Kings 2:9-15**).

Look at Joseph. Before he ran Egypt, he ran a prison. Before he ran a prison, he ran Potiphar's house. He kept serving faithfully in small places until God put him in a palace (**Genesis 39-41**).

Even Jesus came down as a servant, washing feet when He could've been flexing His power (**John 13:1-17**). If the Son of God could take second place, what makes us think we're too good to?

Now let me bring it closer to home. My friend Greg Mauro served evangelist Morris Cerullo for thirty-two years. That's not a typo, thirty-two years faithfully making sure another man's ministry never missed a beat. You think Greg didn't have his own dreams? Of course he did. But he understood something most people don't, there's honor in being second. There's power in loyalty. God sees that kind of faithfulness, even if nobody else claps for it. You can read about it in his book "The Blessing of Serving another Man's Ministry".

Look around, we live in a culture where everyone wants followers, everyone wants the mic, everyone has their own podcast, everyone is writing a book, everyone wants to be "the one." But God is asking, "Can you serve another man's vision before I hand you your own?" Jesus said in **Luke 16:12**, *"If you are not faithful with what belongs to someone else, why should you be trusted with what is your own?"*

So I gotta ask you, are you okay with serving someone else's business, someone else's ministry, someone else's family, while God builds your character? Can you be faithful with no credit? Would you do it for no pay? Can you hold up someone else's arms before God puts a staff in your hand?

For real though, leadership ain't about being famous, it's about being faithful. And sometimes faithfulness looks like being second, learning in the shadows, until God says, "Now it's your turn."

Handle That

- Check your heart, are you serving to shine, or are you serving to learn?
- Pray for the leaders above you instead of criticizing them.
- Find one way this week to honor or support someone else's vision without expecting your name in the credits.

Take Note

- Am I truly okay being second if that's where God has me right now?
- Do I get jealous when others succeed, or do I celebrate them?
- What lessons can I learn in the shadows that will prepare me for the spotlight?

Take It to God

Father, thank You for reminding me that leadership starts in service. Teach me to be like Joshua, faithful even when I'm not in charge. Help me to celebrate others instead of being jealous. Give me the patience to stay in Your presence and learn while I serve. Remove pride and ego from my heart, and let me find joy in helping others win. When my time comes, let me be ready because I was faithful in the shadows. **In Jesus' Name, Amen.**

You Don't Need the Crowd

"Then Moses called for Joshua, and as all Israel watched, he said to him, 'Be strong and courageous! For you will lead these people into the land that the Lord swore to their ancestors He would give them. You are the one who will divide it among them as their grant of land. Do not be afraid or discouraged, for the Lord will personally go ahead of you. He will be with you; He will neither fail you nor abandon you.'" - (Deuteronomy 31:7-8 NLT)

Life and Leadership Lesson

Now picture this moment: Moses, the OG leader, is passing the torch to Joshua. The people are watching. The crowd is there. But Moses is basically saying, "Josh, you don't need all these folks behind you to validate you. What you really need is God going before you". Moses didn't hype him up by telling him the people would always be loyal. Why? Because Moses knew firsthand that crowds turn on leaders real quick. One day they're cheering you, next day they're throwing rocks. Crowds are loud, but they're not loyal. God is steady. And that's the secret Moses was handing Joshua.

Boom, that's the truth. You don't need the crowd, you need the call. You don't need everybody's approval, you need God's presence.." because let's be real, how many of us depend on the crowd? The applause? The likes? The approval? Are you living to be liked, or are you living to be faithful?

See, leadership can get dangerous when you're addicted to validation. If you're leading for the crowd, you'll bend to please them instead of following God. You'll compromise when you should stand firm. You'll get distracted when you should stay focused. The Israelites were proof of that: one minute they were cheering Moses for bringing them out of Egypt, and the next they were talking smack and wanting to go back (**Exodus 14:11-12**). Crazy, right? They complained about food and water (**Exodus 16:2-3, Numbers 20:2–5**). They even wanted to stone him and choose another leader (**Numbers 14:10**). And let's not forget when they built that golden calf while he was gone (**Exodus 32**). That's the same crowd Joshua was about to lead. Moses knew better than to tell him, "Don't worry, the people got your back." He told him, "God's got your back."

Moses tells Joshua, "Be strong and courageous." Notice he doesn't say, "Make sure the people like you," or "Get the crowd hyped." Strength and courage come from God being with you, not from who's around you. **Psalm 118:6** says, *"The Lord is for me, so I will have no fear. What can mere people do to me?"*

David had moments when his own men wanted to stone him (**1 Samuel 30:6**). Think about Jesus, the crowd even turned on him when He started preaching harder truth (**John 6:66**). When He entered Jerusalem, the crowd shouted *"Hosanna!" (Matthew 21:9).* But not long after, that same crowd shouted, *"Crucify Him!" (Matthew 27:22).* If Jesus needed the crowd, He would've folded. But He knew His mission wasn't about their approval, it was about the Father's will. So, if you're gonna lead, you gotta learn to walk without the crowd's approval. Paul went from being praised as a god in **Acts 14:11** to almost being stoned to death in the same chapter. Paul planted churches and still had folks dogging him out. Leaders can't base their mission on the crowd, because the crowd is unstable.

Even Paul said in **Galatians 1:10**, *"If I were still trying to please man, I would not be a servant of Christ."* That's the raw truth. You can't lead both the crowd and the call. You've got to choose.

Leadership ain't about filling arenas, it's about being faithful. Don't get it twisted, the crowd will clap when you benefit them, but the second you challenge them, they'll flip. That's why your confidence can't be in how many cheer for you. It's gotta be in knowing God goes before you.

So whether you're sitting in a cell, running a business, pastoring a small church, raising kids with no applause, or building something nobody sees yet, don't trip. You don't need the crowd. You need His presence. So let me ask you: Are you chasing the applause of people, or are you chasing the presence of God? If the crowd left you tomorrow, would you still move in your calling? Who are you leading for? The crowd or the calling? Are you addicted to applause, or can you keep moving when it's just you and God?

Handle That

Check yourself this week. Are you making decisions for applause or for obedience? Write down one move you've been hesitating on because you're worried about people's opinions. Then take the step anyway, knowing God's with you. Build your confidence in God's presence, not people's claps.

Take Note

- Who am I leading for, the crowd or Christ?

- When was the last time I felt discouraged because of lack of support?

- How can I remind myself that God's presence is enough when I feel alone?

- Where have I been living for approval instead of purpose?

- Ask yourself honestly: "Am I doing this to be seen or because I'm called?"

- How do I respond when people don't support me or believe in me?

- What would it look like to lead boldly, even if no one follows right away?

- Who have I been leading for, the crowd or Christ?

Take It to God

Father, forgive me for the times I've craved the approval of the crowd more than Your approval. Teach me to lead for You, not for applause. Remind me that You go before me and that I don't need the hype to stay faithful. Give me courage when I feel alone, boldness when I feel weak, and peace when the crowd disappears. Thank You that I don't need the crowd to validate me. Remind me that real leadership is not about applause, but about obedience. I admit I like approval. I like the applause and the support. But help me to see that I don't need the crowd, I need You. Give me the courage to lead when it's lonely, the strength to stand when I feel abandoned, and the focus to trust Your promise that You'll never leave me or forsake me. Teach me to lead with my eyes on You, not on the crowd. **In Jesus' Name, Amen.**

Chapter 37

Let the Next Ones Lead

"After the death of Moses the Lord's servant, the Lord spoke to Joshua son of Nun, Moses' assistant. He said, 'Moses my servant is dead. Therefore, the time has come for you to lead these people, the Israelites, across the Jordan River into the land I am giving them." - (Joshua 1:1-2 NLT)

Life and Leadership Lesson

Boom! That's heavy. God straight up said, "Moses is dead. Joshua, you're up." No sugar coating. No warm-up speech. No long farewell tour. Just like that, the baton was passed. And here's the truth, leadership is never permanent. It's seasonal. You might be holding the mic today, but one day someone else will.

And that's why pouring into the next generation is one of the most important things you'll ever do as a leader.

Look at Moses. He didn't just keep the spotlight for himself. He took Joshua under his wing, let him shadow him, let him watch the highs and lows, the Red Sea miracles and the wilderness complaints. Joshua got to see it all. Why? Because Moses was preparing him for the day God would say, "Now it's your turn."

A real leader isn't insecure about raising up the next one. A real leader knows that legacy is more important than spotlight. Think about Jesus. He could have carried the mission solo, but He poured into twelve disciples who carried the gospel to the world. Paul poured into Timothy. Elijah poured into Elisha. If you're not raising up others, what are you really building?

Now let's get personal. Who are you pouring into right now? Your kids? Your employees? Your church volunteers? The younger dudes on the block who look up to you? Or are you so focused on your own grind that you forgot leadership ain't just about you?

Here's what's wild, the next generation doesn't need perfect leaders, they just need some present leaders. Leaders who show up, who share their wisdom, who are honest about their mistakes, who can relate to their pain, and who can be available. Joshua didn't get a perfect Moses, he got a real one. And it was enough to prepare him for his call.

For my business folks, this is about succession. If your company falls apart the day you step away, you didn't build leaders, you built dependents. For my street dudes, this is about the younger homies watching you. Are you teaching them wisdom, or letting them repeat your mistakes? For church leaders, this is about making disciples, not just filling pews.

And let me keep it all the way real, sometimes we don't let the next ones lead because of our own pride. We don't want to be forgotten. We don't want to admit our season might be ending. But think about it. If Moses hadn't prepared Joshua, the people could've been left leaderless. God's work would've moved on, but Moses' legacy might've died.

The next generation needs you, they need you to be the example, they need you to show up. They need your perspective and guidance. I remember the youth pastors that poured into us. I remember the neighborhood dad, Noah Bernardo Sr. pouring into us, taking us to church, playing football with us on Maitland, having bible study at his house, and pointing us to Christ after learning from his mistakes. This Man's actions of leadership changed all of our lives. Who are you doing that for?

So here's the big question: are you building for the now, or are you building for the next?

Handle That

- Identify at least one Joshua in your life, someone younger in faith, leadership, or experience, and start pouring into them consistently.
- Stop thinking you have to be perfect before you can mentor. Share your story, share your scars, share your lessons.
- Ask God to show you who He's raising up around you, and commit to investing in them.

Take Note

- Who has been a Moses in my life?
- Who am I intentionally raising up?
- If God called me home today, would my leadership die with me, or live on through others?

Take It to God

Father, thank You for showing me that leadership is never just about me. Help me to be intentional about raising up the next generation. Show me the Joshuas around me, the people I'm supposed to pour into. Give me the humility to step aside when my season ends, and the courage to prepare others for their season. I don't want my leadership to die with me, I want my legacy to live on through the ones You've trusted me to raise up. **In Jesus' Name, Amen.**

The Mentor in Your Life

"When his father-in-law saw all that Moses was doing for the people, he said, 'What is this you are doing for the people? Why do you alone sit as judge, while all these people stand around you from morning till evening?' ... Moses listened to his father-in-law and did everything he said." - (Exodus 18:14-24)

Life and Leadership Lesson

Moses is the main guy, the face of the movement, the leader in the headlines. Yet when Jethro pulls up, Moses bows, hugs, and brings him into the tent to talk real. That's honor. That's humility. That's teachability. And then Moses does something most leaders avoid. He tells the whole story. Wins and wounds. Victories and hardships. He lets a mentor into the details.

So, who gets to sit in your tent? Who can you be honest with about the good and the ugly? If the answer is nobody, that's a problem. Leaders who have no mentors drift. Leaders who have no mentees go stale. A healthy leader lives in both lanes. You receive wisdom, then you pour wisdom.

Jethro didn't just listen. He watched Moses burn out and said, "This isn't good." He gave structure, not shade, and helped Moses build a team so the people could be cared for and Moses wouldn't collapse. That's what mentors do. They see what you can't see, say what others are scared to say, and show you a better way.

The Bible stays giving us mentor-mentee pairs:

- **Moses and Joshua**. Joshua served in the tent, lingered in God's presence, learned battle and prayer, then stepped into command when Moses was done. **Exodus 33:11, Numbers 27:18-23, Deuteronomy 31**.
- **Elijah and Elisha**. Elisha left his old life, followed close, asked for a double portion, then carried on the work. **1 Kings 19 and 2 Kings 2**.
- **Paul and Timothy**. Paul calls Timothy his true son. He lays hands, stirs gifts, corrects with love, and trusts him with heavy assignments. **1 Timothy 1:2, 4:14, 2 Timothy 1:5-7, 2:2**.
- **Barnabas and Paul**, then Barnabas and **John Mark**. Barnabas vouched for Paul when nobody believed him. Later he took Mark when Paul gave up on him. Years later Paul says Mark is useful. That's restoration in motion. See **Acts 9:26-28, Acts 15:36-39, 2 Timothy 4:11**.
- **Naomi and Ruth**. Wisdom meets loyalty. Naomi guides. Ruth listens and moves with honor. **Ruth 1-4**.

- **Eli and Samuel**. Eli teaches Samuel how to hear God's voice. "Speak, Lord, for your servant hears." **1 Samuel 3**.
- **Mordecai and Esther**. Strategy, courage, timing. Mordecai coaches Esther into purpose for her people. **Esther 4**.
- **Jesus and the Twelve**, with a tighter circle of Peter, James, and John. He lives with them, teaches, corrects, sends, then releases them. **Mark 3:13-15, Luke 9, Matthew 28**.

Crazy, right? Mentorship is not a side quest. It is how God shapes leaders and sustains movements.

Now let's make it personal.

- If you are a street dude trying to build a new life, who is your Jethro that is helping you unlearn old habits and learn new ones?
- If you are a business owner, who can look at your books, your culture, your ego, and tell you the truth before it all cracks?
- If you are a pastor, who can call you out if you start performing instead of praying?
- If you are locked up, who is the older brother pointing you toward wisdom so you come out ready, not bitter?

A real mentor will do four things:

1. **Listen to the whole story** like Jethro. You can be honest, no filter.
2. **Name the problem** without shaming you. "This isn't good." Clear, not cruel.
3. **Offer a God-shaped plan** that serves people and protects your soul.
4. **Point you back to God** so you do not become dependent on them.

A real mentee will do four things:

1. **Honor**. Moses bowed. Respect opens doors that talent cannot.
2. **Tell the truth**. No image management. If you want help, be real.
3. **Obey quickly** when the counsel aligns with Scripture and the Spirit.
4. **Pass it on**. What you learn, you teach. What you receive, you share.

Leaders, hear me. Your longevity is tied to your humility. You cannot disciple nations if you refuse to be discipled as a man. You cannot father teams if you refuse to be fathered. You cannot expect loyalty while rejecting correction. That's wild. Take it easy. Get low so God can lift you.

Also, do not just hunt for a mentor. Be one. Joshua becomes Joshua because Moses made room. Elisha becomes Elisha because Elijah let him walk close. Timothy becomes Timothy because Paul wrote letters, prayed, and sent him. Who are you pouring into? Who is watching your daily faith, not just your highlight reel?

Traits to look for in a mentor:

- Fears God more than people.
- Proven track record in the area you need help.
- Tells you yes and no with the same love.
- Lives what they teach at home, not just in public.
- Keeps confidences. No gossip.
- Points you to Jesus, not to themselves.

Traits to look for in a mentee:

- Teachable. No excuses.
- Faithful in small things.
- Hungry for growth, not clout.
- Honest about weaknesses.
- Ready to serve before they are seen.

One more gut check. Are you trying to be everybody's mentor so you can feel important, but you have no mentor keeping you honest? Or are you always the student but never pouring into anyone else because you feel unworthy? Both are off. Receive and give. Learn and lead. In the tent with Jethro. In the camp with the people. That balance will keep you steady.

Handle That

- Write three names. One mentor you will pursue this month. One peer who can tell you the truth. One mentee you will invest in weekly.
- Text or call them today. Set a real rhythm. Monthly with your mentor. Weekly with your mentee.
- Choose one area to submit to counsel right now: finances, family, purity, schedule, leadership decisions.

Take Note

- Who is allowed in my tent to hear the full story, not just the wins?
- When was the last time I acted on hard counsel and it saved me from a dumb move?
- Who am I actively training to replace me if God says it is time to pass the baton?
- Where do pride and secrecy still block me from being mentored?

Take It to God

Father, thank You for Jethros, for mentors who speak life and correction. Strip pride out of me. Make me teachable. Put the right voices around me and give me courage to obey wise counsel. Show me who to pour into and how to serve them well. Let my leadership be marked by humility, accountability, and fruit that lasts. Raise up a whole line of Joshuas, Elishas, Timothys, and Esthers from my obedience. **In Jesus' Name, Amen.**

Share the Spirit

"Then the Lord said to Moses, 'Gather for me seventy men of the elders of Israel, whom you know to be the elders of the people and officers over them, and bring them to the tent of meeting, and let them take their stand there with you. And I will come down and talk with you there. And I will take some of the Spirit that is on you and put it on them, and they shall bear the burden of the people with you, so that you may not bear it yourself alone." - (Numbers 11:16-17 ESV)

Life and Leadership Lesson

Let's be real for a second. Leadership will break you if you try to do it solo. Moses was out here carrying millions of people on his back, stressed out, worn down, ready to quit. And God told him something wild: "I'll take some of the Spirit that's on you and share it with them." Boom. That's leadership, it's not about hoarding power, it's about multiplying it.

God never designed leaders to carry the load alone. That's why He told Moses to gather seventy elders. Notice what God didn't do, He didn't create a brand-new spirit out of thin air for those elders. Nah, He took what He already gave Moses and spread it around.

That's crazy when you think about it. It means what God gave you isn't just for you. That anointing, that wisdom, that hustle, that favor, it's meant to be shared. Leaders aren't supposed to be hoarders, they're supposed to be distributors.

So let me ask you, are you passing down what God gave you, or are you clinging to it like it's yours? Who are you training, mentoring, discipling, pouring into?

Look around at the Bible. Elijah passed the mantle to Elisha (**2 Kings 2:9-15**). Jesus poured into the twelve, then they flipped the world upside down (**Acts 1:8, Acts 2**). Paul wrote letters to Timothy and Titus, teaching them how to pastor, how to lead, how to guard the faith (**2 Timothy 2:2**). Even Barnabas put Paul on his shoulders when nobody else trusted him (**Acts 9:26-27**).

Here's the problem with a lot of us today, we want to be the star. We want the mic, the followers, the recognition, the spotlight, the awards. But a true leader says, "Nah, let me multiply this. Let me raise someone else up so they can lead when I'm gone."

That's legacy. That's how you build movements instead of monuments.

Think about Joshua again. He started as Moses' assistant, just hanging out at the tent. Moses didn't crush his growth, he let God build him. And when the time came, Moses passed the leadership baton and Joshua carried the people into the Promised Land (**Deuteronomy 34:9**). Moses didn't cling to the spotlight, he shared the Spirit.

Now think about yourself. Are you building people up to keep going when you're not around? Or does everything fall apart if you're not there? That's a leadership gut check right there.

Handle That

- This week, identify one person you can pour into, it could be a younger co-worker, your kid, a guy in your cell block, someone in your church. Teach them one thing God has taught you.
- Stop trying to be the only voice in the room. Invite others to share their wisdom.
- Pray for the courage to let go of control so others can rise.

Take Note

- Who are the "seventy elders" in your life that God is asking you to raise up?
- Am I leading in a way that multiplies, or am I hoarding the influence for myself?
- If I was gone tomorrow, who would carry the work forward?

Take It to God

Father, thank You for reminding me that leadership isn't about me being the only one. Teach me to share the Spirit, to pour into others, and to trust that You'll multiply what You've put in me. Show me who to raise up, who to mentor, and who to trust with the load. Help me let go of pride and control, and let me lead in a way that leaves legacy, not just noise. **In Jesus' Name, Amen.**

Chapter 38

You Were Built for This

"Now Joshua son of Nun was full of the spirit of wisdom, for Moses had laid his hands on him. So the people of Israel obeyed him, doing just as the Lord had commanded Moses." - (Deuteronomy 34:9 NLT)

Life and Leadership Lesson

Crazy, right? Joshua didn't walk into leadership by accident. He was built for it. He had been in training all along. Walking behind Moses. Watching. Learning. Carrying the weight before ever carrying the title. By the time Moses was gone, Joshua wasn't just next in line, he was prepared.

That's how God works with leaders. You don't just get dropped into the spotlight cold. God builds you in the quiet places. In the battles no one else saw. In the moments of serving faithfully when it looked like nothing was happening. You were built in the fire, not in the comfort.

Look at David. Before he was king, he was a shepherd boy fighting lions and bears in the field. Before Joseph ran Egypt, he was in prison managing other prisoners. Before Peter preached to thousands, he was a fisherman cleaning nets. Boom! That's wild, God always builds His leaders before He reveals them.

So let me ask you, what battles are you in right now that feel pointless? What struggles are you going through that make you question if you're even on the right path? Could it be that God is building you in ways you don't even see yet?

For the entrepreneur grinding at 2 a.m., the inmate wondering if their life still has purpose, the pastor questioning if their ministry is making a difference, the parent trying to hold it together, hear me: you were built for this. God doesn't waste seasons. That pain, that trial, that waiting room moment, that court case, that layoff, it's not random. It's preparation. Thats your wilderness.

Joshua was filled with wisdom because Moses laid hands on him. That's transfer. That's discipleship. That's mentorship. You don't get everything just from books or YouTube sermons, you get it from walking with people of God who pour into you. Who are your Moses figures? And even deeper, who are you laying your hands on to prepare for tomorrow?

And here's something to chew on: leadership ain't easy. There will be haters, doubters, betrayals, and heavy nights. But if God says you were built for it, then no storm, no prison cell, no financial collapse, no sickness can cancel that. **Romans 8:37** says we are **"more than conquerors through Him who loved us." Philippians 1:6** reminds us that **"He who began a good work in you will bring it to completion."**

The enemy will try to tell you you're not enough. That you don't have the education, the resources, the connections, or the background. But tell me this, since when did God pick leaders who were "qualified" by man's standards? Moses stuttered, David was overlooked, Rahab had a past, Peter denied Jesus. And yet, God still said, "You're built for this."

So I'll flip it on you: do you believe you're built for what God has called you to? Or are you still letting fear or shame hold you back?

Handle That

- Write down three battles or seasons you've gone through that God may have used to build you.
- Identify one mentor who's poured into you, and thank God for them, and then Thank them personally.
- Identify one person you can start pouring into right now.

Take Note

- Where has God been preparing me without me realizing it?
- Do I truly believe I was built for this? Why or why not?
- What step of faith is God asking me to take right now?

Take It to God

Father, thank You for building me even when I didn't see it. Thank You for using the pain, the losses, and the waiting to shape me into who I am today. Help me to remember that You built me for a purpose bigger than myself. Give me the courage to step into that purpose, and the humility to prepare others for theirs. Remind me daily that I am not alone, because You are with me every step of the way. **In Jesus' Name, Amen.**

Learning from Those Before Us

"Then Joshua secretly sent out two spies from the Israelite camp at Acacia Grove. He instructed them, 'Scout out the land on the other side of the Jordan River, especially around Jericho.' So the two men set out and came to the house of a prostitute named Rahab and stayed there that night." - *(Joshua 2:1 NLT)*

Life and Leadership Lesson

Crazy how Joshua learned from the past. Moses had sent out **twelve spies** into the land (**Numbers 13**), but ten of them came back with fear and doubt, talking about giants and how they looked like grasshoppers. That whole generation missed out on the promise because fear spread faster than faith. But Joshua? He was one of the two that believed. So now, years later, when it was his turn to lead, he wasn't gonna make the same mistake. He only sent **two**. Boom! That's wisdom right there.

Don't get it twisted, this chapter right here is about learning from those who came before us. Joshua wasn't just moving blind. He had lived through history. He saw Moses send twelve spies into the promised land back in **Numbers 13**. Ten came back trippin', spreading fear and doubt. They were shook about giants, talking about *"we look like grasshoppers in their eyes."* And what happened? That fear infected everybody, the whole camp melted down, and an entire generation missed out on the promise.

But Joshua? He was one of the two who said, "Nah, with God on our side we got this." Years later, when it's his turn to lead, Joshua wasn't about to make the same mistake. He learned from what he saw under Moses. Instead of sending twelve spies, he sent two. Less mouths, less drama, less fear to spread.

That's wisdom. That's strategy. That's leadership.

Let's be real, how many times have you seen somebody else fail and then went ahead and repeated their same mistake? Be honest. How many times have you ignored the warning signs and thought you'd be different, but ended up falling into the same pit? Leadership means paying attention to what went wrong before, owning it, and adjusting. The second time around hits different if you learn from what went wrong the first time.

Think about it: Joshua sending only two was like saying, "I don't need a crowd, I just need the right ones around me." He was selective. That's a lesson right there. Leaders don't just move fast, they move wisely. Who you send matters. Who you trust matters. Your circle matters.

And peep this: the two spies end up in Rahab's house. Out of all the people they could've connected with, God linked them to a prostitute. Yes, a prostitute. That's wild. That's God's way of reminding us that He uses unlikely people to play key roles. Don't trip if your help comes from a place that looks messed up to the world. Don't underestimate the Rahabs in your life. God might send somebody you'd least expect to be the very one who covers you, protects you, and points you toward your next step. Rahab plays into this too. That's wild. It shows us that God will use unlikely allies when you're on mission. Don't count people out. The second time around might come with help from someone you never expected.

Look at Peter. He denied Jesus three times (**Luke 22:61-62**). But the second time around, after the resurrection, Jesus restored him and told him, *"Feed my sheep"* (**John 21:15-17**). That failure became fuel for his future. Paul? He used to persecute the church, but the second time around, after meeting Jesus, he built the church (**Acts 9**). Jonah ran the other way, but the second time around, God gave him another shot to preach in Nineveh (**Jonah 3:1-2**).

History isn't just a story, it's a manual. Leaders who ignore it are doomed to repeat it. Joshua shows us you don't have to. Joshua wasn't reckless. He didn't just say, "We'll wing it this time." Nah, he got strategic. He remembered what happened under Moses' watch, and he tightened up the plan. Boom! He paid attention to history, owning the mistakes, and still moving forward.

So let me ask you: what have you learned from those who went before you? The second time around is about growth. It's about learning from mistakes, adjusting the game plan, and not letting history repeat itself. How many times have you blown it the first time? You tried to start a business and it failed. You tried to get clean and you relapsed. You tried to fix your marriage and it fell apart again. Maybe you even tried leading before and got burned. But check this out: failure ain't final. The second time around can hit different if you take the lessons with you.

Think about your life. What's your "second time around" moment? Maybe you're locked up right now, and God's giving you a second chance to walk different when you get out and allow others to see what God has done in your life. Maybe you're in business, and the first venture tanked but now you're wiser. Maybe you're in ministry, and the first time you rushed it, but now God's refining you in the waiting. The question is, are you learning from the past, or are you just repeating the cycle?

The second time around is proof that God ain't done with you. Learn from failure and the wisdom of trying again.

Handle That

- Stop beating yourself up over what went wrong the first time. Write down three lessons you learned.
- Don't just repeat the past. Adjust your strategy. What will you do differently this time?
- Identify your "Rahabs", those unexpected people God may have positioned to help you.
- Don't just repeat the past, adjust. What can you do different this time?

Take Note

- What's the "giant" that made me quit the first time?
- Am I walking into my second chance with faith, or am I dragging the same fear with me?
- Am I approaching my second chance with faith or with fear?
- Who in my circle can I trust to walk with me into this second round?

Take It to God

Father, thank You that You are the God of second chances. Forgive me when I ignore lessons from the past or repeat mistakes that should have taught me better. Teach me to lead like Joshua, with wisdom, strategy. Open my eyes to the Rahabs You've placed in my path. Help me walk into my second chance with faith, not fear, and lead others with boldness and humility. Forgive me for the times I let fear or failure stop me. Teach me to lead with wisdom, and to trust that You are with me in the second time around. Show me where You're opening doors again, and give me the courage to walk through them. **In Jesus' Name, Amen.**

Sometimes We Don't Finish What We Start

"From the mountaintop you will see the land from a distance. But you may not enter the land I am giving to the people of Israel." - (Deuteronomy 32:52 NLT)

Life and Leadership Lesson

That one hits heavy. Moses, the man who led millions out of slavery, the man who parted seas, the man who met God face to face, didn't step foot into the Promised Land. Crazy, right? After all that, he only got to see it from a distance.

That should wake us up as leaders. Sometimes, even with all our grind, our faithfulness, our sacrifice, we might not be the ones to finish what we started. And you know what? That's okay. Because leadership is never about *you*, it's always been about serving, about the mission, about the people, and ultimately being the example that Jesus was, and pointing it all back to God.

Think about David. He had the vision to build the temple, but God told him no, that it would be his son Solomon's job **(1 Chronicles 28:2-6)**. David laid the foundation, Solomon finished the job. John the Baptist? He preached repentance, baptized Jesus, and got things ready, but it was Jesus who brought salvation **(John 3:30)**. Paul planted churches all over, but he admitted in **1 Corinthians 3:6**, *"I planted, Apollos watered, but God gave the growth."*

So let me ask you, are you okay with the possibility that your job is to start something, but someone else will finish it? Or does your pride need the credit?

This is especially for leaders, pastors, entrepreneurs, parents, or even a guy in a prison cell dreaming of a second chance. Maybe your role is to plant the seed, and someone else gets to see the fruit. Maybe you grind to build a business your kids will take to another level. Maybe you lay down a foundation in ministry that the next generation will run with. Maybe you mentor someone who'll out-preach, out-lead, or outshine you, and that's not failure, that's legacy.

Moses didn't enter the land, but his fingerprints were all over it. Every stone, every tribe, every law, every leader, all of it carried Moses' influence. That's the beauty of leadership. You don't always need to cross the finish line yourself to know you ran your race. **Hebrews 12:1** says we are running a race, but it's not always about speed or glory, it's about faithfulness.

Now, here's the raw truth: some of us may not finish things because of disobedience. Moses struck the rock in anger **(Numbers 20:11-12)** instead of following God's instruction. Leaders, our actions matter. Our attitudes matter. Our obedience matters. You can't lead in anger, bitterness, or pride and think it won't cost you. But here's the flip side, even when Moses messed up, God still let him see the land. That's grace. That's God saying, "You may not cross, but you're still my servant, and I'm still keeping my promise."

So what about you? What's God asking you to start? And are you willing to accept that maybe your role is to prepare the way for someone else? Are you okay with being the one who starts the movement, but not the one who finishes it?

That takes humility. That takes trust. That takes understanding that the Kingdom is bigger than your ego.

Handle That

- Ask yourself honestly: do I need to always get credit, or am I willing to play my role faithfully, even if I don't finish the project?
- Write down one thing you've started that you might need to hand off to someone else.
- Pray over the next generation of leaders who will finish what you started.

Take Note

- Am I faithful to the mission, or just to my own recognition?
- What's one area of my life where I've been frustrated about not finishing?
- How can I shift my perspective to see legacy instead of loss?

Take It to God

Father, thank You for trusting me to carry what You've given me, even if I'm not the one to finish it. Help me to lead with humility, to plant faithfully, and to build with legacy in mind. Teach me to let go of the need for credit, and to focus on obedience. Remind me that even if I don't see the final result, You are still faithful to complete the work. **In Jesus' Name, Amen.**

Chapter 39

It's Not About You, It Never Was

"And Moses said to the people, 'Fear not, stand firm, and see the salvation of the Lord, which He will work for you today. For the Egyptians whom you see today, you shall never see again. The Lord will fight for you, and you have only to be silent." - (Exodus 14:13-14 ESV)

Life and Leadership Lesson

Let me keep it all the way real with you, leadership was never about you. It ain't about the claps, the likes, the spotlight, or even the titles. It's about obedience to God and service to people.

Look at Moses at the Red Sea. He didn't step up to flex like, "Watch what I can do." Nah. He said, "Watch what God is about to do." That's the heart of real leadership. Pointing people to God, not yourself.

And man, I had to learn this the hard way. I'll be straight up, I used to crave the credit. I loved being the guy behind the scenes working with artists, athletes, big names, because part of me wanted to hear, "Yo, Ruben made that happen." But you know what? That pride will eat you alive. There were times I worked on projects and didn't get my name mentioned at all. No credit, no shoutout, not even a "thank you." And I remember feeling salty, like, "Man, I did all that and y'all can't even acknowledge me?"

But that's when God whispered, "It's not about you." Boom. Conviction hit.

There was a time I was serving at a church in Modesto and I was asked if I would volunteer at a men's meeting and assist the pastor with a few things on stage. I was honored. I felt noticed by this particular Pastor.

I showed up ready to serve, ready for whatever God wanted to do. Me and my mentor, Bo Herroz, got our instructions. But the vibe shifted. No acknowledgement from the pastor. No hello, no handshake, no eye contact. Nothing.

Honestly, I straight up felt disrespected. I shut my mouth and went about the assignment given to us but I did it with a sour face. I mean, I wasn't looking for a shoutout from the stage or anything, just to be acknowledged. It's our human nature to want to be appreciated. I didn't feel that way at all and you can tell in my demeanor.

Afterward, Bo approached me, "Bro, what's wrong with you? You ain't your self.". I explained that we acknowledge people where we come from, and I don't like being treated like I'm invisible, the pastor never even acknowledged me the entire time and I ain't the one!

I can tell he was disappointed about my reaction. He shook his head and went on to say, "Bro, are you really worried about recognition from a man? You want to be acknowledged by that guy? That's all? Because if all you want is a pat on the back from man then that's all you will get! Why did you even come tonight? To be noticed, or to serve?" He then reminded me, "you need to check the posture of your heart when you serve. Why are you really doing this? Where's your heart at? You gotta do all this unto the Lord and don't worry about anyone around you!"

Ouch. It stung, but I needed it. That correction stuck with me. Now I repeat it everywhere I go: check your heart when you serve. If you serve for applause, that's all you'll get. If you serve for God, He sees it, even when nobody else does. **Colossians 3:23. Matthew 6.** Do it in secret. Let God keep the receipts. Take it easy.

Same thing with Love Thy Neighbor. I've been in spots where we pulled off big community events, helped families, gave away resources, and sometimes other people tried to swoop in and get the spotlight. For a second, I wanted to fight for my recognition, but then I remembered, we don't do it for the applause. We do it because people matter and because God called us to. When I got that in my heart, I found freedom.

Here's the truth: if you're always chasing recognition, you'll burn out real quick. But if you serve out of obedience, you'll keep going even when nobody notices. As a servant leader you're supposed to eat last, be the first one to show up and the last one to leave. It's never about power and being in charge, it's about taking responsibility *and* taking the blame. It's not about a title, it's about being an example and being a servant. It's about doing what needs to get done without worrying about who gets the credit. And that's leadership.

Moses modeled that. John the Baptist modeled that when he said, "He must increase, but I must decrease" (**John 3:30**). Paul said it too, "So neither he who plants nor he who waters is anything, but only God who gives the growth" (**1 Corinthians 3:7**). Even Jesus, the Son of God, said, "The Son of Man came not to be served but to serve, and to give His life as a ransom for many" (**Mark 10:45**). If Jesus Himself was cool with serving without credit, who are we to chase applause?

Let me ask you something personal: do you only serve when people notice? Do you get frustrated when nobody thanks you? Are you more focused on being seen or on being faithful?

Because here's what I've learned, the real applause comes from God. And His "well done" means more than a thousand likes on social media or a pat on the back from the crowd.

So stop stressing about credit. Stop making it about you. Because it never was. It's about God and the people He called you to serve.

Handle That

- Write down one area where you know you've made it about yourself. Be real with yourself.
- Flip it. Ask: "How can I make this about God and others instead?"
- This week, do one act of service in secret. Don't post it, don't tell nobody. Just do it for God.

Take Note

- What bothers you more: not being noticed, or not being obedient?
- How do you usually react when you don't get credit?
- What would change in your leadership if you fully embraced the truth that it was never about you?

Take It to God

Father, thank You for reminding me that leadership ain't about me. Forgive me for the times I chased credit, clout, or recognition. Teach me to lead like Moses, John the Baptist, Paul, and Jesus, humble, focused, and servant-hearted. Help me decrease so You can increase. Let me care more about obedience than applause. Remind me that the only "well done" that matters is Yours. In Jesus' Name, Amen.

Lead by Faith

"It was by faith that Moses, when he grew up, refused to be called the son of Pharaoh's daughter. He chose to share the oppression of God's people instead of enjoying the fleeting pleasures of sin. He thought it was better to suffer for the sake of Christ than to own the treasures of Egypt, for he was looking ahead to his great reward. It was by faith that Moses left the land of Egypt, not fearing the king's anger. He kept right on going because he kept his eyes on the one who is invisible. It was by faith that Moses commanded the people of Israel to keep the Passover and to sprinkle blood on the doorposts so that the angel of death would not kill their firstborn sons. It was by faith that the people of Israel went right through the Red Sea as though they were on dry ground. But when the Egyptians tried to follow, they were all drowned." - (Hebrews 11:24-29 NLT)

Life and Leadership Lesson

Here's the truth: Moses' whole leadership was built on faith moves. Every major step he took was crazy in the natural, but he trusted God. That's why Hebrews lists him up as an example.

Let's break down just some of the faith plays Moses made:

- **By faith he left the palace.** He gave up comfort, riches, and security because he believed God's people were his people. That's leadership, stepping into pain when you could hide in luxury.

- **By faith he faced Pharaoh.** Think about that, he went back to the place he ran from after killing a man, and stood toe-to-toe with the most powerful ruler alive. Pharaoh had an army, chariots, and power. Moses had a stick and God's word. Guess who won?

- **By faith he lifted his staff over the Nile.** When the water turned to blood (**Exodus 7**), it didn't happen because Moses had some power in his stick. It happened because he trusted God enough to look crazy doing what God said to do.

- **By faith he kept obeying through the plagues.** Every time Pharaoh hardened his heart, Moses kept showing up. Most of us would've quit after the first "no." Leaders don't stop at rejection, faith keeps knocking on the same door until it opens.

- **By faith he introduced Passover.** Imagine telling people to kill a lamb, smear blood on their doors, and believe that death would pass them by. That's wild. Yet Moses believed and taught the people to believe. Leaders don't just have faith for themselves; they train others to walk in it.

- **By faith he stretched his hand over the Red Sea.** Everyone else was panicking, crying, ready to die. God told him to move, and he stepped up, raised his staff, and watched God split the ocean. Leaders move in faith when others freeze in fear.

- **By faith he struck the rock and water came out (Exodus 17).** The people were ready to stone him. They were thirsty, angry, and doubting. Moses still trusted that God could bring provision out of a rock in the desert.

- **By faith he climbed Sinai alone.** Think about it, he went up the mountain into the fire, thunder, and smoke when everyone else stayed back in fear **(Exodus 19).** That was faith to draw near to God when it was terrifying.

See the pattern? Moses' whole leadership wasn't about being the smartest, the strongest, or the most polished. It was about having the faith to do what God said even when it didn't make sense. That's what separates leaders who make history from leaders who fade away.

So let me ask you:

- What palace are you refusing so you can walk in your purpose?
- Who's your Pharaoh, and do you believe God will give you the words when it's time to speak?
- What Red Sea is in front of you, and are you willing to raise your hand in faith while everyone else doubts?
- Are you teaching your people: your kids, your crew, your team, to trust God the way Moses taught Israel?

Faith isn't just about believing in your head. Faith moves your feet. Moses didn't just say he trusted God, he acted like it. Hebrews says, "By faith he kept going." Leaders today gotta do the same.

Handle That

- Identify one Pharaoh in your life (a challenge, fear, or opposition). Write down how you're going to face it in faith this week.
- Take a step of faith that looks crazy but you know God's calling you to do it.

Take Note

- What's your "Red Sea" moment right now?
- How can your faith set the example for others to follow?

Take It to God

Father, thank You for showing me through Moses that leadership is built on faith. I don't want to lead by fear, insecurity, or pride. Teach me to trust You the way Moses did, to walk away from comfort, to face opposition with courage, and to obey when it doesn't make sense. Strengthen my faith so that others can walk through doors I open by trusting You. Let me lead in such a way that people say, "God was with him." **In Jesus Name, Amen.**

Chapter 40

From Moses to the Messiah

"Suddenly, Moses and Elijah appeared and began talking with Jesus. Peter exclaimed, 'Lord, it's wonderful for us to be here! If you want, I'll make three shelters as memorials, one for you, one for Moses, and one for Elijah.' But even as he spoke, a bright cloud overshadowed them, and a voice from the cloud said, 'This is my dearly loved Son, who brings me great joy. Listen to him." - (Matthew 17:3-5 NLT)

Life and Leadership Lesson

Boom, here it is. The whole book has been about Moses, but the truth is this, Moses was never the finish line. He was a shadow pointing to the real thing. A setup for the main act. When Jesus hit the scene, He didn't just pick up where Moses left off, He fulfilled what Moses couldn't.

Moses gave the Law, but Jesus brought grace and truth (**John 1:17**). Moses led people out of slavery in Egypt, but Jesus leads people out of the slavery of sin (**Romans 6:6**). Moses lifted a bronze snake so people could live, but Jesus lifted up His life on a cross so the whole world could be saved (**John 3:14-15**).

Think about that. As powerful as Moses was, God Himself had to say on the mountain, *"Listen to Him."* Meaning stop camping out with the messenger and follow the Messiah. How many of us still camp out around leaders, movements, traditions, or even ourselves, instead of truly listening to Jesus?

Let's keep it real, leaders, pastors, bosses, parents, influencers, all of us, we're just middle-men. At best, we're the road signs pointing to Jesus. The trap is when we start thinking the sign IS the destination. Like Peter, we build tents around experiences or people when God is trying to show us the Son.

Ask yourself: who's the real leader in your life? Who are you listening to above all? Your homies? Your bank account? The streets? That insecurity that won't shut up in your head? Or are you actually tuning in to Jesus?

Leaders, business owners, fathers, mothers, pastors, coaches, all of us need to hear this. Your influence ain't about you, it's about who you're leading people to. If it stops with you, it dies with you. But if you point people to Jesus, that legacy lives forever.

Think about John the Baptist, he had crowds, influence, attention. But he said *"Behold, the Lamb of God who takes away the sin of the world"* (**John 1:29**). His whole job was to point to Jesus. That's the blueprint.

And let's not forget Paul, that dude had every reason to boast in himself, yet he said, *"Follow me as I follow Christ"* (**1 Corinthians 11:1**). He wasn't building disciples for himself, he was building them for Jesus.

So, the lesson? As leaders, your role is important, but you're not the center. As my wife always reminds me…It's not about your name on the flyer, your title on the business card, your name in bright lights, or how many likes or followers you get online. It's about whether people see Jesus through you.

Sometimes we just get it twisted. We are on a never ending quest to become the best versions of ourselves, when we are just supposed to be reflections of Jesus.

That's the difference between Moses and Jesus. Moses was drawn out. Moses pointed you to the law, Jesus fulfilled it. Moses delivered, Jesus saves. Moses showed the way, Jesus IS the way.

Handle That

This week, check your leadership. Are you pointing people to yourself or to Jesus? Be real about it. Don't let ego get in the way of God's glory.

Take Note

Write down three ways you can shift the focus off yourself and put it back on Jesus in your leadership. Where have you been hogging the spotlight, and how can you redirect it?

Take It to God

Father, thank You for reminding me that it's not about me, it's always been about Your Son. Help me lead with humility, always pointing people to Jesus and not myself. Forgive me for the times I've made it about my name, my platform, or my pride. I want my life and *unlikely leadership* to be a reflection of Jesus, the true Messiah. Keep me centered, focused, and surrendered to Him. **In Jesus Name, Amen.**

The Real Leader We Follow

"And so, dear brothers and sisters who belong to God and are partners with those called to heaven, think carefully about this Jesus whom we declare to be God's messenger and High Priest. For he was faithful to God, who appointed him, just as Moses served faithfully when he was entrusted with God's entire house. But Jesus deserves far more glory than Moses, just as a person who builds a house deserves more praise than the house itself. For every house has a builder, but the one who built everything is God. Moses was certainly faithful in God's house as a servant. His work was an illustration of the truths God would reveal later. But Christ, as the Son, is in charge of God's entire house. And we are God's house, if we keep our courage and remain confident in our hope in Christ." - (Hebrews 3:1-6 NLT)

Life and Leadership Lesson

Boom, let's talk real. Moses was legendary. He freed a whole nation, talked with God face to face, split seas, and pulled off miracles that would put Hollywood blockbusters to shame. But even with all that, Moses wasn't the main event. He was the setup man. The spotlight was always pointing toward Jesus.

And that's the trap a lot of us fall into. We start putting our ultimate trust in people. Your pastor, your boss, your favorite motivational speaker, or even your own ability. But let's be real, every human leader eventually slips up. Moses got angry and hit the rock when God told him to speak to it (**Numbers 20:11**). David was called a man after God's own heart, but he fell into adultery and murder (**2 Samuel 11**). Peter was bold, but he denied Jesus three times (**Luke 22:61-62**). Even the best leaders have cracks in their armor.

So the question is, who are you following when your leader falls short? Who's your foundation when the pastor stumbles, when the CEO crashes the company, when the influencer you looked up to gets exposed? If your trust is in people, your faith will rise and fall with them. But if your faith is in Jesus, you got a leader who never fails, never leaves, and never loses.

Peep this, Moses led the people out of Egypt, but Jesus leads us out of sin. Moses lifted up his staff to open a sea, Jesus lifted up a cross to open the gates of heaven. Moses prayed on the mountain for the people, Jesus intercedes right now at the right hand of the Father for you (**Romans 8:34**). That's next level leadership.

Now think about leadership in your own life. Are you trying to be the savior for everybody? Are you carrying pressure like you're supposed to fix it all? Let me remind you, you're not the Messiah. Our job as leaders is to point people to Jesus, not to ourselves. John the Baptist said it best in **John 3:30, "He must increase, I must decrease."** That's the posture of a real leader.

Leaders inspire, but Christ transforms. Leaders point the way, but Christ is the way. Leaders open doors, but Christ IS the door (**John 10:9**). Leaders can give advice, but Christ gives eternal life.

So ask yourself right now: who's really leading you? Is it your emotions, your money, your mentor, your homies? Or is it Jesus? And if you're leading others, are you pointing them to Him, or are you just pointing them to you?

Handle That

This week, humble yourself. Remember you're not the final stop, you're just the sign pointing to Jesus. Lead your family, your business, your crew, your church, but always point back to Him.

Take Note

Write down two places in your life where you've been relying more on people than on Jesus. Then write down how you can shift that focus back to Him.

Take It to God

Lord, thank You for showing me that no leader is greater than Your Son. Help me respect and honor the people You place in my life, but never put them above You. Teach me to lead like Moses, but always remember that Jesus is the one true leader. Keep my heart humble, keep my eyes fixed on Christ, and let my leadership point others back to Him. In Jesus Name, Amen.

Moses Led Them Out, But Jesus Leads Us In

Moses led the people out of Egypt, out of slavery, out of bondage. But Jesus? He leads us into freedom. He leads us into life. He doesn't just break chains, He gives you a new name.

Moses gave the Law - Jesus fulfilled it. (**Matthew 5:17**)

Moses spoke to God on behalf of the people. - Jesus is God, speaking to you directly.

Moses held up his staff to part the Red Sea - Jesus held up a cross to part death and sin.

"For the law was given through Moses; grace and truth came through Jesus Christ." - (John 1:17)

Pointing Back to Jesus

This chapter, like this whole book, is not about Moses. It's not even about me. It's about Jesus, the One who takes broken, unqualified, uncertain, unlikely people and says, **"You're exactly who I want."**

Jesus is greater than Moses. Moses delivered people from physical slavery. Jesus delivers us from spiritual bondage. So whatever bush God is calling you from, listen. Lean in. And don't be afraid to say, **"Here I am."**

Jesus Chose the Unlikely to Lead

Look at who Jesus called:

- Fishermen. (**Matthew 4:19**)
- A tax collector. (**Luke 5:27**)
- A woman at a well with a reputation. (**John 4**)
- A violent man named Saul who became Paul. (**Acts 9**)

Not one of them had it all together. But all of them were down to follow Him. So the question isn't: "Am I good enough?" The real question is: Will you say yes?

Final Lessons

As we wrap, let me leave you with some takeaways:

- It's ok to start late, Moses was 80 when he really stepped into purpose.
- It's ok to not be seen, God sees you.
- It's ok to fall, Just don't stay down.
- Real leaders serve.
- It's ok to feel unqualified, because the call is never about what you bring to the table... it's about what He's already put in your hand.

One Last Question: Do You Know Jesus?

If you've made it this far, you didn't just want leadership lessons. You wanted something deeper. Maybe your heart's been stirred. Maybe you've been running from the call on your life. Maybe you're just tired of doing it your way and you're ready to surrender.

Keep it real yo! Jesus is the only reason I'm alive today. He changed me. He called me. He kept me. And He's calling you right now.

Right Where You Are

If you're ready to give or rededicate your life to Jesus… If you're ready to stop running… If you're ready to step into purpose… Pray this from your heart:

Jesus, I believe You are the Son of God. I believe You died and rose again for me. I've made mistakes. I've tried to do it my way. But today, I surrender. Come into my life. Lead me. Use me. I want to follow You. In Jesus' name. Amen.

Now What?

If you just prayed that, welcome to the family. You're not alone. You've got a story now. A testimony. And if you're already walking with Jesus, let this be a reminder: Stay humble. Stay available. Stay surrendered. Lead like Moses, but live for Jesus. Because at the end of the day, this whole book was never just about Moses… It was about how God uses flawed leaders to point people to the flawless One.

Let's go. - Ruben Torres

Here's what people say about Ruben

Ruben...To Me..A brother, friend, confidant..Someone I trust to tell me what I need to hear when I need to hear it..Even when I don't like it..As Genuine as they Come..Blessed to have him in My Life. - **Paco Mansin, Childhood friend/ Musician**

The word "pillar" gets thrown around a lot when describing important, significant figures in the world and in our local communities. But, I can say without exaggeration that Ruben is exactly that: A pillar in the San Diego community. A pillar is not always noticeable, flashy, or self-promotional. They often carry the weight of responsibility and leadership quietly and consistently, working behind the scenes to make their community a better, stronger, and safer place to be.

I believe Ruben's contributions to the San Diego community and to the next generation are unparalleled, and his impact extends far beyond the natural and into the supernatural. Ruben has been a significant, God-sent blessing to our ministry, Revive-All USA, but more importantly, he has also become a good friend to me personally. I believe this new book, "The Moses Factor" will help many people discover Biblical leadership as well as healing in their own journeys and stories. **- Jordan Lunderville, Evangelist and Founder of Revive All USA**

"Ruben is a true leader of men. That's how I've always seen you, bro!" - **Ernie EROCK Dorame, Musician**

"Ruben Torres is not only a pioneer in the entertainment industry but also a game changer and catalyst for successful artists and the underprivileged." - **Johnny Murillo, Chicano Hollywood**

Over the past decade it's been a true blessing to walk alongside Ruben, sharing both laughs and tears. His bold faith, humility, and heart for people always shines. He's more than a leader to me, he's the big brother I never knew I needed. - **Guillermo "Memo" Urrea, Connected Podcast Co-Host, The Good Merc owner**

"Ruben Torres truly represents what it means to lead by serving others. His unwavering dedication to making a positive impact on the community, along with his unique ability to bring people together for a common good, is genuinely inspiring." - **Miguel Rodriguez, Start up Specialist**

"When it comes to leadership, Ruben is always a step ahead of the game. Disciplined, strategic, servant-minded, and humble, yet strong and courageous. Ruben has been able to harness all the best qualities of leadership in one complete package." - **Pastor Mark Porter**

"You're a man who has endured a lot of obstacles in life and is still fighting. It takes courage and lots of obedience, and I admire you as a man who does not give up." - **Jorge Agiss, Business Owner**

"Ruben has been a great role model for the community. He's always finding ways to give back. We appreciate and respect him." - **Rkeyzz, Musician**

"Ruben Torres is a leader and a visionary, like an unstoppable train." - **Daniel Servioj, Photographer**

"When I think of Ruben Torres, immediately GRIT comes to mind. He's resourceful and creative when it comes to getting a vision launched. Ruben is my guy!" - **Lamar Lacagñan, Musician**

"The heart and soul Ruben exemplifies for the neighborhood is unmatched. It takes a leader like him to transform communities." - **Carlos Nicasio, Entrepreneur**

"I want to say Ruben Torres is a true man of GOD. He helps whenever he can and is a blessing to many. After doing 15 years on a life sentence, Ruben helped me get my first job and driver's license, even though he didn't know me. I'm grateful to GOD for putting him in my path." - **Richie Leon, Community member**

"Be the change you want to see in others. A man of faith sees through the darkness. This is what I see in my brother Ruben!" - **Enrique Rivera, Musician/Artist**

"Ruben Torres embodies authenticity and transparency, two keys to building trust in leadership. He leads without pretension or self-promotion, making him someone others can follow with confidence and passion." - **Paul Morales, Executive Producer, Mor Creative Films**

"In the short time I've known Ruben, I've been inspired by his generosity, kindness, and genuine desire to help his neighbor." - **Andy Jimenez, Musician**

Life isn't worth much if you are not able to be a blessing and love on thy neighbor! That's how I see Ruben Torres - **Elias Cordero - Ruben's Homie**

"Having known Ruben since childhood, it's been a privilege to see him grow from a kid into a man, husband, father, and a pillar of the community. His loyalty, humility, compassion, and commitment to his passions inspire others to serve and a great man to follow." - **Chuck Quandt, Southtown Original**

"There is no better person to write a book on leadership than Ruben Torres. He leads with God in his heart and always brings out the best in people." - **Robert Moreno, Community Leader**

"I have experienced Ruben's constant passion to inspire others for many years. His leadership over various endeavors is a testimony of his amazing heart for others." - **Gary Beneventi, Pastor-Chief Operating Officer New Vision Church**

"Ruben has been a mentor to me long before we ever met, his actions and selfless service inspired me to rise higher as a man and as a leader. Today, I am honored to call him not only my mentor but my brother. The Moses Factor is a testament to his life's calling, reminding us that love, leadership, and faith are the true foundations of greatness." **Chris Lv Leyva, Film maker**

He who follows well, leads well...for leadership is the fruit of faithful following. - **Ron "THA KUYA" Galido, Man of God**

Ruben is an inspiration to many in the community, especially in South Bay. He has a humble heart to serve others and sacrifices for the Kingdom of GOD. - **F-cer, Musician**

I'm honored to call Ruben Torres a brother , a friend and a mentor. He's an incredible husband, father, and community role model. Ruben's heart for leadership and his authenticity inspire those around him and the community. He's one of my favorite people, and I'm grateful for his impact in my life... Ahuevo! - **DJ Beto Perez**

A true example of leading by example. Even through the thickest of times, his deep faith has kept him and those around him well grounded. - **Tim Hernandez, Photographer**

For anyone in the middle of a battle, the best person to hear from is someone who has fought and seen victory through many of their own. Ruben is an example for any believer who needs encouragement for God to make a way when it looks like there isn't one. I am honored to call him my friend and privileged to endorse this book that I know God will use to touch your life and current circumstances. - **Pastor Toby Bowker**

Ruben Torres is definitely a leader and a person who goes above and beyond to give back to others and his community. He is probably one of the few who tries to connect others within his community, so everyone wins and doesn't ask for much in return. His success with his non-profit, Love Thy Neighbor proves his work continues to succeed every year. He is a San Diego Legend and if you don't know now you do. Boom! - **Tim Testa, Community member**

With a heart like Moses, Ruben has shown us that true leadership is not about personal gain, but about serving others and lifting them up. Those arms of love have extended across the border by him being a blessing and making an impact in our community here in Tijuana, Mexico. - **Junior on the Beat, Blessed Studios Producer, Tijuana Baja California, Mexico**

"From the streets of San Diego to the pages of this book, Ruben's journey echoes the story of Moses: chosen in weakness, empowered by God. The Moses Factor is a fresh call for leaders, innovators , and disciples to trust that God can still use their lives for His glory." "Ruben shows us that leadership is born in the wilderness. This book is proof that God still uses the unlikely." - **Pastor Ariel Dela Peña, Rock Church, San Diego**

The year I got saved in ' 96, I met Ruben Torres. Since that day, we connected and we've done big things together, and he still is going strong because of the love for Christ. If you know Ruben, he will do anything for you, trust me I know. He is one of my best friends. **- Pastor Dennis Martinez, former World Champion Skater**

Ruben Torres; It's an honor to know you friend- A steadfast family man, community leader, and humble servant of the Lord; 1 Peter 5:6 - **Oscar Amado, SDPD**

Ruben Torres is a lifelong friend and one of the most genuine people I know, someone whose heart is always set on serving others. He's consistently stood up for causes that many overlook, quietly putting in the work where it matters most. In my book, that kind of selfless commitment defines real impact. - **DJ Mikeski Degracia - San Diego Music Pioneer**

"Ruben Torres was one of the first people who inspired me to get involved in my community. Through his faith, leadership, and the incredible events he's created, he showed me what it looks like to serve with heart and purpose." - **Francisco "Frank" Salazar, Community Activist & Youth Mentor**

Ruben Torres is a mover and shaker in a world who actually lives out the big talk hustle. Whether doing community ministry or pouring into those around him with years of experience and wisdom, Ruben is a "Real One" in a sea of fakes. The Moses Factor will tap into knowledge and help you be a better leader and world changer. - **Justin Sarachik Editor-in-Chief Rapzilla.com, Manager of Rapzilla Artists, & Author of Survival of the Artist**

Ruben has gifted our generation with a much needed reminder of what God can do with a surrendered heart regardless of its past and limitations. Whether you are a young adult with little life experience and spiritual knowledge or a biblical scholar broken by a lifetime of failures, "The Moses Factor" helps evoke the call that remains the same. The ones that will be used to love, lead, and be a light in the world, will be the ones who despite yesterday's setbacks & failures will accept each morning's new grace and continue to do the work that many have been called to, but few will do. - **Gerry Skrillz, Musician**

About the Author

Ruben Torres is a creative director, community organizer, and founder of the *Love Thy Neighbor Movement*, a grassroots organization that bridges faith, culture, and community across San Diego and Tijuana. Born in Tijuana and raised in South San Diego, Ruben's journey from the streets to serving others has shaped his purpose and voice.

He's worked in music, film, and outreach - from producing music and videos to leading toy drives, youth programs, and peace gatherings that bring hope where it's needed most. His work has been recognized by the City and County of San Diego with an official *"Ruben Torres Day"* in his own hometown.

Known for his real-talk approach and street-level faith, Ruben's message is simple: **you don't have to be perfect to be called, just willing.** Through *The Moses Factor* and his ongoing work, Ruben continues to challenge people to show up, serve others, and walk in their God-given calling.

Get Involved

Partner with us to support more ministry events, correctional facility outreaches, podcast productions, and the connected men's retreat.

www.lovethyneighbormovement.com

IG @ltnmovement

CONNECT WITH RUBEN TORRES

IG @connectedwithrt

www.ingramcontent.com/pod-product-compliance
Lightning Source LLC
Chambersburg PA
CBHW051503150726
47997CB00001B/90